MW00979826

judgment

against the gods

gerald c mclean

judgment

against the gods

Copyright © 2008 by Gerald C. McLean

ALL RIGHTS RESERVED
No portion of this publication may be reproduced, stored in any electronic system, or transmitted in any form or by any means, electronic, mechanical, photocopy, recording, or otherwise, without written permission from the author. Brief quotations may be used in literary reviews.

Cover art by Andrew McLean

All Scripture quotations are taken from the King James Version of the Bible. Scriptures will appear in italics. Bold type will be added at times for special emphasis in some Scriptures and selected quotes.

ISBN: 978-0-9816349-0-6
First Printing: April 2008 – 1,000 copies

FOR INFORMATION CONTACT:
Gerald McLean
djmenugu@aol.com

Printed in the USA
By Morris Publishing
3212 East Highway 30
Kearney, NE 68847
800-650-7888

dedication

Since truth can be lost in a single generation,
I dedicate this book to my children Andrew, Brian,
and Heather and to my children's children Josiah,
Seth, Ethan, and Mahala
that they might serve the God of their father
with all of their heart, mind, and soul!

acknowledgements

A doctrinal book is born out of the accumulation of knowledge derived from a multitude of sources. I must begin by thanking my teachers— foremost among them my pastor, Rev. Frank Tamel of Oak Creek, Wisconsin. This great man of God taught by example the importance of studying God's Word and of loving truth. Through their writing ministries and lectures, Rev. David Bernard of Austin, Texas; Rev. David Huston of Carlise, Pennsylvania; and Rev. Dr. Trevor Neil, Fort McMurray, Alberta, Canada have been extremely influential in my understanding of the Godhead. I also want to thank my theology instructors from Gateway College of Evangelism—men who taught me to search the Scriptures—Rev. Jacob Nelson, Florissant, Missouri; Rev. Dr. Arlo Moehlenpah, Chula Vista, California; Rev. W. C. Parkey, Poplar Bluff, Missouri; and the late Rev. Paul Dugas.

My thanks to those who helped review the original manuscript and offered their suggestions to make it a better book. This group included Rev. Darlynton Jakin, Enugu, Nigeria, West Africa; Rev. David Huston; and Rev. Frank Tamel.

My thanks to my son Andrew McLean, Potts Camp, Mississippi, for designing the cover and offering technical support.

My thanks to John and Kristin Contino, Milwaukee, Wisconsin, for proofreading the manuscript.

My thanks to those who encouraged me to follow through on this project—most notably Rev. David Huston and Rev. Jerry Richardson, Saint Charles, Missouri.

My thanks to my beloved wife Darla for the layout work, formatting, and technical support.

And most of all, thanks to my Lord and Savior Jesus Christ for revealing the truth of the Mighty God in Christ to me.

Gerald C. McLean

foreword

In forty years of Christian ministry, I have read a lot on Christology and I hasten to say that once I started to read Missionary Gerald McLean's book, "*Judgment Against the Gods*," I couldn't put it down. It is incredibly and captivatingly good—a truth lover's treat.

Writing from Nigeria in the heart of Africa, McLean has had numerous encounters with the gods that reside in the sincere minds of believers that are mistakenly wrong. Gerald McLean knows that the true God will not share His glory with another and is not afraid to unmask tri-theism that sometimes masquerades as a confusing three-gods-in-one package. Many contend they believe in one God but refuse to concede that there is "none other." McLean's book removes that mystery.

Bishop Frank Tamel
Parkway Apostolic Church
Oak Creek, Wisconsin

table of contents

preface

Do we need another book on the Godhead? I think not. We already have the most authoritative Book on the subject that was ever written, the Bible. Unfortunately man has wrested the Scripture to his own destruction throughout the history of the Church Age. This manipulation of Scripture, often reflecting the views of philosophers and pagans more clearly than holy men of God as they were moved by the Holy Ghost, has led to an inordinate amount of confusion and false doctrine relative to the teaching on the Godhead. Although there have been many far more capable writers on this subject—David Bernard, David Huston, Frank Ewart, Brent Graves, T. B. Neil and Fred Kinzie come to mind immediately—another perspective may help lead someone to a saving knowledge of the Mighty God in Christ. That is the purpose of this book.

Raised as a Roman Catholic, I was far more knowledgeable about the dogma of the Catholic Church and its catechism than I was about the Bible. My early understanding of God was shrouded in mystery and ritual. Unquestioningly I adhered to the doctrinal teaching of a triune God and made sure that I didn't slight one of the three Persons in the Godhead when I went to God in prayer.

In my mid teens a friend invited me to attend a Pentecostal Church service. This was definitely a taboo, but I reasoned one visit couldn't hurt. It didn't. I left that service mortified by the "antics" of the people—the shouting, hand clapping, dancing, and tongue talking. The well meaning brother who tried

1

to force me to the altar (for what, I didn't know) sealed the deal. I was gone. Two years would pass before I would make a second visit to that same church, and even I wasn't sure why I agreed to making the same "mistake" twice. Two more years would elapse before I made a third visit to the church. This time, as the songwriter proclaimed, "Something got a hold of my heart and it wouldn't let me go."

Some weeks later, sitting in the basement of a house with some 14 other teenagers between the ages of 15 and 19, I had my first experience where I felt God spoke directly to me. The occasion for the gathering was a home Bible study. As previously noted, my knowledge of the Bible at this time was practically non-existent. I didn't know the difference between the Old Testament and the New Testament. I couldn't understand why the Books of the Bible were laid out in such "haphazard" fashion. It would have been far easier to find the Bible texts referred to in church and Bible study if the Books had been arranged in alphabetical order. When I got my first Bible I thought the last Book of the Bible was Concordance!

At any rate when the Bible study began, we all turned to Genesis 1:1. I read, *"In the beginning God created the heavens and the earth."* My life instantly changed. God assured me at that very moment that all Scripture was given by the inspiration of God and that every word in this great Book was true. Although even a rudimentary understanding of Scripture was still in the future for me, I did have an assurance that even if I didn't understand something that I read in the Bible, it was still true.

As the years unfolded, I began to study God's Word with earnestness and my darkened eyes were opened to so many of the great issues of life--the greatest of which is the Bible teaching of God's absolute Oneness.

The Oneness of God as revealed throughout the pages of the Old Testament and ultimately in Christ in the New Testament is the Supreme Doctrine of the Bible. All other doctrines are secondary to the understanding of this great truth. As my Pastor, Rev. Frank Tamel, so often proclaimed, "If you are wrong about the identity of Christ, nothing else really matters." Jesus is God and beside Him there is no other.

I will set out to prove this in a systematic way using the Bible as my primary resource. Let the Bible speak for itself. *"Let God be true and every man a liar" (Romans 3:4).*

The title of the book, *Judgment Against the Gods,* is taken from Ex 12:12, *"For I will pass through the land of Egypt this night, and will smite all the first-born in the land of Egypt, both man and beast; and **against all the gods of Egypt I will execute judgment**: I am the LORD."* God judged the false gods of the Egyptians and God will one day judge all the other false gods of man's imagination. God will also judge those who misrepresent the One True God as a triune god (a false doctrine that has polluted the truth of God's Word since the 2nd Century).

Provocative? Yes, it is meant to be. Subtle? No. It is strong meat and, if you are easily offended and are afraid to look at the facts for fear that they may get in the way of your beliefs, perhaps this is not the book for you. For the willing, it should serve as a reminder to all generations that God is a jealous God and that He will not share His glory with another (Exodus 20:5, Isaiah 48:11). One day every knee will bow and every tongue will confess that Jesus Christ is Lord (Isaiah 45:23, Philippians 2:10). One day there will be an ultimate judgment of the gods!

1 what is truth?

Pontius Pilate asked Jesus, *"What is truth?"* *(John 18:38).* Truth was standing right in front of Pilate. Jesus was the visible manifestation of Truth (John 14:6). Yet Pilate's pride, tempered by his political standing, social upbringing, religious ignorance, and humanistic educational background, would not allow him to accept Truth. Even though he was warned by God through his wife's dream not to touch this man, Pilate dismissed Truth because it didn't come packaged in a way consistent with his perceptions of Truth. How many other people over the centuries have come face to face with Truth, but have brushed Him aside because it was not expedient or consistent with previously held beliefs?

To answer the question, "What is truth?" one must look to the Words of Jesus. Jesus said, *"I am the Truth" (John 14:6).* Jesus said, *"If you continue in my Word, then are ye my disciples. And ye shall know the truth, and the truth shall set you free" (John 8:31-32).* Jesus said, *"Thy Word is Truth" (John 17:17).*

Jesus was proclaiming, in essence, that since God cannot lie (Hebrews 6:18) and since God does not change (Malachi 3:6 and Hebrews 13:8), then truth, which comes from God, is absolute. Since God is Truth and since God doesn't change, then truth is not relative; it does not or cannot change.

There was a time when mankind taught and believed that the world was flat. There was a time when mankind did not believe that men would ever fly. If a man rejects the notion that there is a law of gravity, does it undo the law of gravity? The world was always spherical, man has become airborne, and the law of gravity exerts its presence everyday, with or without a man's belief or consent. Truth is truth no matter what a man believes. Truth is not contingent on the masses believing or the endorsement of learned men. Truth stands whether one man, one million men, or no men believe.

"Thy Word is Truth" (John 17:17). That settles it. The Word of God is the final authority. The Word of God repeatedly teaches and proclaims that God is One. Proverbs 23:23 shouts with authority, *"Buy the truth and sell it not...."* The admonition is clear; the truth is not for sale at any price! That fact will never change.

It doesn't matter how some men view the Godhead, it is already settled in God's Word. *"Hear O Israel: the LORD our God is one LORD" (Deuteronomy 6:4)*. The Scriptures identify God as the "Holy One" fifty-two times. God is referred to as the "Just One" two times. The Word of God states "God is One" three times and that there is only "One God" seven times. It is settled. God is One. He is not three in one, He is One. That is what the Word of God says.

How Does Man Form His Impressions of God?

In a 2002 seminar, lecturer, author, and Bible scholar, David Huston, addressed a group of ministers in Ibadan, Nigeria. As he opined on peoples' perceptions and conclusions about the nature of God, he concluded that those perceptions and conclusions were the result of imagination, tradition, revelation, or a combination of the three.

For the last 11 years I have lived in Nigeria while serving as a missionary. During this time I have seen numerous idol houses and false gods made of wood or stone and ornamented with all manner of baubles. Food is often offered to these "gods"—gods that are incapable of thought or activity, let alone the ability to eat. Depending on the village or tribe, some Nigerians believe that trees, monkeys, or pythons house ancestral spirits and are revered as messengers of the gods or gods themselves. The marine god is enshrined in Nigerian tribal folklore. Where did these ideas about God originate? They are the product of man's fertile imagination, and have permeated an entire culture. Most would agree that man's imagination should not be the birth place of God nor should it be the source of our knowledge of God.

Others have gleaned their perceptions of God in denominational churches. They have been taught certain dogmas, creeds, and traditions that have been handed down from generation to generation and in some cases from century to century. There is typically little questioning of these church positions because most members in these churches are "won" into the church through birth or by their parents. The unspoken rule in these homes and churches is that if it was good enough for father and mother, and grandfather and grandmother, then it is good enough for me. Since these dogmas, creeds, and traditions are so ingrained in the fabric of the church and in the minds of the people attending said churches, there is almost no challenge as to where certain beliefs or practices arose. Some church bodies will even agree that certain denominational doctrines and practices have no biblical basis, but argue that church dogma and tradition are equal to the Bible. This opens the door for all sorts of extra-biblical teaching and gives much latitude for the perpetuation of false or non-biblical doctrines.

Man's imagination will not lead him to God nor will church dogma or creeds. Imagination is conjecture at best and many traditions and most creeds are based upon unsound exegesis. That leaves only one way to find out about God, through revelation. Revelation comes from the Word of God. *"The entrance of thy words giveth light; it giveth understanding unto the simple" (Psalm 119:130).* The Word of God draws back the curtain of darkness and reveals the mysteries of God to us. To safeguard us against false doctrines based upon man's dreams, visions, philosophies, or traditions, Peter proclaimed,

"We have also a more sure word of prophecy; whereunto ye do well that ye take heed, as unto a light that shineth in a dark place, until the day dawn, and the day star arise in your hearts: Knowing this first, that no prophecy of the scripture is of any private interpretation. For the prophecy came not in old time by the will of man: but holy men of God spake as they were moved by the Holy Ghost" (II Peter 1:19-21).

What Peter was trying to convey in his second letter to the Church was that although he was eyewitness to one of the greatest revelations ever beheld by man, the Transfiguration of Jesus Christ, he did not preach or teach about his dreams, visions, or use cunningly devised fables when proclaiming the gospel—not even the Transfiguration! He underscored the fact that his preaching and teaching relied on the *"more sure Word of prophecy,"* which is the Word of God.

To understand the Godhead, one must go to the Supreme source of revelation, the Bible. Even Jesus proclaimed, *"Sanctify them through thy truth: thy word is truth" (John 17:17).*

When Jesus was tempted in the wilderness, Jesus overcame the temptations by quoting God's Word. Considering that Jesus was God and that anything He would have said would have been the Word of God, He certainly did not have to quote Scripture to overcome the temptations He was facing. But He purposely quoted Scripture to underscore the credibility of the written Word and its Supreme place in our lives not only as overcomers, but also in doctrinal formulation.

God wants us to know Him and understand Him. *"But let him that glorieth glory in this, that he understandeth and knoweth me, that I am the LORD which exercise lovingkindness, judgment, and righteousness, in the earth: for in these things I delight, saith the LORD" (Jeremiah 9:24).* The Godhead is no longer a mystery; it has been revealed to us through the Word of God. *"And without controversy great is the mystery of godliness: God was manifest in the flesh, justified in the Spirit, seen of angels, preached unto the Gentiles, believed on in the world, received up into glory" (I Timothy 3:16).* The Apostle Paul encapsulates in these few words the essence of the mystery of Godliness. Jesus is God!

2 the progressive self-revelation of god

Today, even in most third world countries, the Bible is readily available to believers. It is hard for us to imagine a world without a Bible. In fact, most of us have several Bibles. Yet there was a time in the history of man when there were no Bibles. From the dawn of Creation to the reception of the Ten Commandments by Moses on Mt. Sinai, there was no written Word. Moses did not write the Pentateuch until approximately 1450 B.C. During the approximately 2,000 years prior to the first appearance of God's written Word, God revealed Himself to man through an audible voice, theophanies, signs and wonders, and through His names, titles, or roles.

"In the beginning God created the heavens and the earth" (Genesis 1:1). In the first verse of recorded Scripture, we are not given God's name. God simply identifies Himself as "God." The word God, in this verse, comes from the Hebrew word Elohim. We learn 3 things about God or Elohim from Genesis 1:1. God is, God is the Creator, and God gave us time.

In Genesis 2:7, God is designated as LORD God. LORD comes from the Hebrew word *Yahweh,* and is represented in English by all upper case letters. This designation of God is given in relationship to God's creation of man. Unlike God's other creative activities in Genesis 1, God does not speak man into existence, but He forms man from the dust of the ground and breathes into his nostrils the breath of life. LORD or Yahweh (Hebrew) or Jehovah (English) then refers to God's special relationship with man and was used accordingly throughout the pages of the Old Testament.

For example, Genesis 15:1-2 reads, *"After these things the word of the LORD came unto Abram in a vision, saying, Fear not, Abram: I am thy shield, and thy exceeding great reward. And Abram said, Lord GOD, what wilt thou give me, seeing I go childless, and the steward of my house is this Eliezer of Damascus?"* Notice that in this passage, when addressing God, Abram uses the title "Lord" as opposed to the previous "LORD" of Genesis 2:7. The Hebrew word for "Lord" is Adonai and means Master. Abram had a revelation that God was not only Creator and that man was the special creation of the LORD, but that God was equally our Master.

Genesis 17:1 reads, *"And when Abram was ninety years old and nine, the LORD appeared to Abram, and said unto him, I am the Almighty God; walk before me, and be thou perfect."* Abram had another revelation from God. God identified Himself as Almighty God or, in the Hebrew, El-Shaddai. Abram now had an understanding that God was Almighty and that there was nothing too hard for Him. Based upon the previously revealed titles of God, Abram had discovered a significant additional fact about the God he was called to serve. His God was Almighty. This may not seem to be significant or earth-shaking to us, but the Patriarchs had no Bible from which to glean information about the nature of God. Their understanding of God came almost entirely through the progressive revelation of His name.

In each of these instances man was learning more about God through His revealed names, titles, and roles. Note that the titles "God" and "Lord" are also applied to gods other than the God of the Bible. In the case of "Lord," this word is occasionally applied even to men. Exodus 32 identifies the object of Israel's worship, the golden calf, as "our god." Similarly the gods of the pagans were identified by the word "god." For instance Baal-Berith (Judges 8:33), Chemosh (Judges 11:24), and Dagon (Judges 16:23) were all identified by the word god or *elohim*. Significantly, even though *elohim* is a plural noun, the aforementioned pagan gods were numerically one. In the Hebrew language, the word *elohim* denotes plurality of attributes and majesty in reference to God, not plurality of persons.[1]

Likewise, even today men hold titles such as "landlord" or "lord of the manor." Obviously then, the words "God" and "Lord" are not names for God, but rather they express something about His character, nature, power, and authority.

When God revealed Himself to Abraham as Jehovah-Jireh in Genesis 22:14, Abraham's understanding of God was further expanded. The Jehovahistic Compounds of the Old Testament continued to present God in a new and ever expanding light to His people. (Jehovah is the English rendering of Yahweh.) Each Jehovahistic Compound added a new perspective of understanding. These compound names revealed God's great desire to play a personal role in the lives of His people. The Jehovahistic Compounds added clarity to man's understanding of God's character, nature, power, and authority. The specificity of the Jehovahistic Compounds accomplished in a deliberate and predetermined way what God could not do by using just the more ambiguous titles of God or LORD.

Compound Names of Jehovah

Jehovah-jireh
Scripture: Genesis 22:14
Meaning: The LORD will provide

Jehovah-rapha
Scripture: Exodus 15:26
Meaning: The LORD that heals

Jehovah-nissi
Scripture: Exodus 17:15
Meaning: The LORD our banner

Jehovah-m'kaddesh
Scripture: Exodus 31:13
Meaning: The LORD that sanctifies

Jehovah-shalom
Scripture: Judges 6:24
Meaning: The LORD our peace

Jehovah-sabaoth
Scripture: I Samuel 1:3
Meaning: The LORD of hosts

14

Jehovah-elyon
Scripture: Psalm 7:17
Meaning: The LORD most high

Jehovah-raah
Scripture: Psalm 23:1
Meaning: The LORD my shepherd

Jehovah-hoseenu
Scripture: Psalm 95:6
Meaning: The LORD our maker

Jehovah-tsidkenu
Scripture: Jeremiah 23:6
Meaning: The LORD our righteousness

Jehovah-shammah
Scripture: Ezekiel 48:35
Meaning: The LORD is present

Imagine the joy the Old Testament saints must have felt when they realized God was a healer, a provider, and an ever present help in time of need. Imagine their sense of security as they recognized God to be their Banner, Peace, and Shepherd. God covered them in His glory and cloaked them in holiness and righteousness. These facts came to the knowledge of the people of God through the progressive revelation of God's name throughout the pages of the Old Testament.

By no means do the above names and titles form an exhaustive list of Old Testament designations for God. For example, further study would disclose that God was also revealed as *El-Elyon,* or the

Most High God (Genesis 14:18); *El-Roiy,* or the God of Sight (Genesis 16:13); *El-Olam,* or Everlasting God (Genesis 21:33); JAH, as a derivative of Yahweh (Psalm 68:4); and Jehovah, or Yahweh (Exodus 6:3). God is the Creator, the Captain of our Salvation, the Lawgiver, our Redeemer, our Shepherd, the Ancient of Days, the Righteous Branch, and the Holy One. This additional list is not exhaustive either, but it does help to further illustrate the point that all the names and titles used for God in the Old Testament describe one and the self same God.

---

[1] R. Brent Graves, *The God of Two Testaments,* (Word Aflame Press, 2000) pp.28-29.

3
judgment against the gods

God called Abraham out of a world of idolatry. In fact, Terah, Abraham's own father, was an idolater (Joshua 24:2). Abraham lived in the thriving metropolis of Ur of the Chaldeans and, as such, had been exposed to multiple false gods through the rampant practice of idol worship. Most notably, the Chaldeans were ignicolists or worshippers of fire.[1] They likewise were astronomers and were well known for the construction of ziggurats: places built for the express purpose of planetary and other celestial body worship. The city god of Ur was the moon god Nannar.[2] When God called Abraham out of Ur, Abraham was not only instructed to leave the place of his nativity, but was also commanded to separate from his pagan family members.

God's plan for Abraham was to make him the father of a great nation; one completely independent of idolatry. It was equally His plan to raise a people that would worship only the One True God.

Although there was a gulf of thousands of years between Abraham and the Apostle Paul, Paul would likewise instruct the early Christian converts in the Corinthian Church to separate themselves from idolatry and from those who practiced the same.

"*Be ye not unequally yoked together with unbelievers: for what fellowship hath righteousness with unrighteousness? and what communion hath light with darkness? And what concord hath Christ with Belial? or what part hath he that believeth with an infidel? And what agreement hath the temple of God with idols? for ye are the temple of the living God; as God hath said, I will dwell in them, and walk in them; and I will be their God, and they shall be my people. Wherefore come out from among them, and be ye separate, saith the Lord, and touch not the unclean thing; and I will receive you, And will be a Father unto you, and ye shall be my sons and daughters, saith the Lord Almighty*" (II Corinthians 6:14-18).

By the conclusion of the Book of Genesis, there are four generations of One God believers: Abraham, Isaac, Jacob, and Joseph. When Joseph was sold into slavery and ultimately ended up in Egypt, he did not forsake the God of his fathers, but acknowledged to Pharaoh that only the One True God could give him the accurate interpretation of his dream (Genesis 41:16). After being elevated to second in command in Egypt, Joseph gave all the glory to the One God of Abraham, Isaac, and Jacob for his exaltation and ultimate success as an administrator in Pharaoh's service. In Genesis 45:5-8, Joseph underscored the obvious: it was the God of his fathers that brought him into Egypt for the preservation of his people. Even though he had spent his entire adult life in Egypt, Joseph proved to his brethren that he had not become an Egyptian when on his death bed he command them to take "my bones from here" when you return to the Promised Land (Genesis 50:22-26). Joseph did not want his body to remain in a land steeped in paganism and idolatry. He wanted his bones relocated to the place where God would make His name known to His people.

Moses Desires to Know the One True God

After the Israelites had relocated to Egypt to escape the famine in Canaan, they became comfortable in Egypt and nested there for some 400 years. When a new Pharaoh took the throne of Egypt who knew not Joseph (Exodus 1:8), and was therefore not beholden to him, the persecution of the Jews in Egypt began in earnest (Exodus 1:11). First, they were enslaved. This was followed by beatings, deprivation, increased work loads, and ultimately their male babies were required at the hands of the Egyptians (Exodus 1:16). As Pharaoh intensified the persecution of the Israelites, the children of Israel multiplied (Exodus 1:12). This only served to further enrage Pharaoh.

The account of Moses has been rehearsed for centuries by Jews and Christians alike. Exodus 2 records how Moses was delivered from certain death by the actions of his godly mother, Jochebed, who fashioned a bulrush ark for baby Moses. As the ark floated along on the river's current, Pharaoh's own daughter collected the ark and adopted the baby that she knew her father had commanded to be killed. God did not just save Moses: he saved him for a purpose. So God arranged to have Moses nursed by his own mother. This gave Jochebed the opportunity to *"train up her child in the way he should go" (Proverbs 22:6)*. Moses may have been schooled by the Egyptians, but his mother anchored him to the faith of the singular God of Abraham, Isaac, and Jacob. The writer of the Book of Hebrews concurs:

"By faith Moses, when he was come to years, refused to be called the son of Pharaoh's daughter; Choosing rather to suffer affliction with the people of God, than to enjoy the pleasures of sin for a season; Esteeming the reproach of Christ greater riches than the treasures in Egypt: for he had respect unto the recompence of the reward. By faith he forsook Egypt, not fearing the wrath of the king: for he endured, as seeing him who is invisible. Through faith he kept the passover, and the sprinkling of blood, lest he that destroyed the firstborn should touch them. By faith they passed through the Red sea as by dry land: which the Egyptians assaying to do were drowned." (Hebrews 11:24-29).

As a young man Moses killed an Egyptian in a misguided attempt to gain the trust of his Hebrew brethren (Exodus 2:11-12). He soon found himself on the outside looking in. Not trusted by the Hebrews and hunted by Pharaoh, Moses retreated to the back side of a desert where he had 40 long years to learn about patience, humility, faith, and trust in God. Ultimately his "Bible school graduation" took place at a burning bush (Exodus 3) where he was given his first job assignment. God called upon Moses to lead the children of Israel out of Egyptian bondage.

A humbled Moses was reluctant to answer God's call to service. His objections were numerous: who am I to lead your people (Exodus 3:11), the people won't listen to me (Exodus 4:1), I'm not a good public speaker (Exodus 4:10), and send someone who is more qualified (Exodus 4:13). But Moses was chosen by God and his excuses were insufficient to alter God's plan for his life.

During the burning bush experience, Moses asked God a most pertinent question: "What is your name?" The conversation went like this:

"And Moses said unto God, Behold, when I come unto the children of Israel, and shall say unto them, The God of your fathers hath sent me unto you; and they shall say to me, What is his name? what shall I say unto them? And God said unto Moses, **I AM THAT I AM***: and he said, Thus shalt thou say unto the children of Israel,* **I AM** *hath sent me unto you. And God said moreover unto Moses, Thus shalt thou say unto the children of Israel, The LORD God of your fathers, the God of Abraham, the God of Isaac, and the God of Jacob, hath sent me unto you: this is my name for ever, and this is my memorial unto all generations" (Exodus 3:13-15).*

God responded with an emphatic and singular expression, **"I AM THAT I AM."** This is significant. Although *"I AM THAT I AM"* is not a name, it is a further revelation of the One True God as the Self Existent One. It established God's numeric oneness using dramatically clear language. This declaration was the bedrock doctrine of ancient Judaism. God is One was, without dispute, the fundamental creed of the children of Israel (Deuteronomy 6:4).

Notice that God did not respond, "We Are That We Are." If the Godhead was plural in number or tri-une in nature, God should have answered Moses' question by saying, "We Are That We Are," or perhaps "We Are the Three in One God." But God deliberately identified Himself as the singular God of Abraham, Isaac, and Jacob.

Moses was directed by the great I AM to prevail upon Pharaoh to let the children of Israel go and worship God. *"And afterward Moses and Aaron went in, and told Pharaoh, Thus saith the LORD God of Israel, Let my people go, that they may hold a feast unto me in the wilderness.* **And Pharaoh said, Who is the LORD**, *that I should obey his voice to let Israel go? I know not the LORD, neither will I let Israel go"* (Exodus 5:1-2).

Pharaoh's response to Moses was pitiful, yet understandable. Pitiful because he did not know the LORD God of Israel; understandable because he was awash in the gods and goddesses of the Egyptians—by some counts over 2,000 of them! If something moved, lived, breathed, made noise, or displayed power, it somehow became part of the religious experience of the Egyptians. Pharaoh was surrounded by images and idols. In fact, Pharaoh even believed that he was a god. By contrast, Moses was asking Pharaoh to let the Israelites worship one God: the LORD God, the great I AM. Pharaoh's skepticism and sarcasm were palpable. He was completely unfamiliar with a singular concept of God, especially of a God that had no image and no name!

The ten plagues that were poured out on Pharaoh's Egypt were not the arbitrary acts of a capricious God who had a prolific imagination; these plagues specifically targeted the major false gods of the Egyptians. *"For I will pass through the land of Egypt this night, and will smite all the firstborn in the land of Egypt, both man and beast; and **against all the gods of Egypt I will execute judgment**: I am the LORD" (Exodus 12:12).* The ten plagues were a judgment against the gods and the false religious system of the Egyptians. Following is a self explanatory list.[3]

Plague 1: Water turned into blood
False God Being Judged: Osiris
Reference: Exodus 7:20

Plague 2: Frogs
False God Being Judged: Hekt
Reference: Exodus 8:6

Plague 3: Lice
False God Being Judged: Seb
Reference: Exodus 8:17

Plague 4: Flies
False God Being Judged: Hatkok
Reference: Exodus 8:24

Plague 5: Cattle disease
False God Being Judged: Apis
Reference: Exodus 9:6

Plague 6: Human sickness (boils)
False God Being Judged: Typhon
Reference: Exodus 9:10

Plague 7: Hail and fire
False God Being Judged: Shu
Reference: Exodus 9:24

Plague 8: Locusts
False God Being Judged: Serapia
Reference: Exodus 10:13

Plague 9: Darkness
False God Being Judged: Ra
Reference: Exodus 10:22

Plague 10: Death of the firstborn
False God Being Judged: All gods and Pharoah
Reference: Exodus 12:29

One of the chief gods of the Egyptians was Osiris, the Nile River or marine god. When the LORD God of Israel turned the water of Egypt into blood during the first plague, it was a calculated attack on Osiris. Imagine the pervasiveness of this plague. All water was turned into blood. The rivers and streams ran red with blood. The wells and springs gushed forth blood. When the tap was opened, blood came out. When one dipped into the water bucket, blood came out. The dew was blood and even the puddles were blood. The stench of death saturated the air as death overtook the water ways. The LORD God proclaimed that He was the real marine God and, as such, He could turn water into blood at the command of His Word. Undoubtedly most Egyptians would never worship Osiris again.

When frogs invaded Egypt during the second plague, the frog goddess Hekt was the specified target. When the Egyptians walked, they had to walk on frogs. They slept with frogs. They bathed with frogs. They sat on frogs. They ate with frogs. Frogs covered the streets, the fields, the floors, the tables, the cupboards, and the beds. They couldn't escape the frogs! Kermit the frog may be cute, but there was nothing cute about this invasion of frogs. The slip, slide, squish, and slime were sickening. The God who created frogs flooded Egypt with one of the objects of their affection until they loathed frogs. Then they begged for frog removal. How many Egyptians would ever have the stomach to worship a frog goddess again?

Plagues three and four were leveled at Seb, the earth god, and Hatkok, the wife of Osiris. These two plagues equally made a mockery of the Egyptian priesthood who prided themselves on their cleanliness. The priests were so fastidious about cleanliness that they went to the extreme of removing all body hair. Now lice blanketed Egypt and even the priests could not escape contamination. With every breath they inhaled lice. Lice invaded every nook and crevice. When the flies came, they were most likely of the blood sucking variety. Egypt was experiencing an all out attack on their belief system and their sanity. Neither Seb nor Hatkok could intervene on behalf of the suffering masses. In the end there was only One God powerful enough to erase the plagues: the I AM That I Am.

Plague five struck at the heart of the Egyptian economy and Apis the bull god. Cattle were relied upon to plow the fields and provide milk, while camels, donkeys, and horses made up the transportation system of Egypt. The One God of Israel executed judgment against the bull god, Apis, and by doing so decimated the Egyptian economy.

The medicine god, Typhon, was unable to hold back plague six. The Egyptians were infected with boils, pus filled, open, running sores that tormented the people. The plague was akin to leprosy with all its attendant pain and horror. Typhon was unable to heal or bring relief. Judgment day had come for Typhon. The God of Israel showed He not only had power to bring disease, but, unlike Typhon, He had the power to heal disease.

Plagues seven and eight were mounted against the gods of Shu, the supposed god of the atmosphere, and Serapia, the god who supposedly protected Egypt from locust infestations. What crops the hail and fire of plague seven didn't destroy, the locusts devoured in plague eight. Judgment day had come for Shu and Serapia.

When darkness fell on Egypt in plague nine, it was against the highest ranking god of the Egyptians, Ra, the sun god. Imagine darkness so thick that it could be felt. Imagine darkness so intense that even the sun could not penetrate it. Neither a candle nor fire could erase the inky blackness of night. For many who feared the dark, this must have been their worst nightmare. How many must have "cracked" under the crucible of impenetrable blackness? Judgment day for Ra had come. The God who created the sun was also able to block it out. The real Sun God had exercised His power in one last attempt to bring the Egyptians and Pharaoh to a place of repentance. But it wasn't to be.

When the death angel passed over Egypt in the tenth plague and all the first born of man and beast were slain, God executed a final judgment against all the gods of the Egyptians. The LORD God proved that He alone was the giver of life and that He could take life away whenever He wanted; there was no one or no assemblage of gods that could stop Him.

The LORD God of Israel had judged the gods of the Egyptians. In dramatic fashion He let them know that the gods of man's imagination, the gods of man's philosophical design, and the gods of man-made traditions are no gods at all. The plagues decimated the religious system of the Egyptians, as well as their country, and it reinvigorated the Israelites to return to the worship of the One True God of their fathers.

One day there will be a judgment of all the false gods of the world. In that day *"every knee will bow and every tongue will confess that Jesus Christ is the One True God" (Philippians 2:10).*

[1] *Adam Clark Commentary*, PC Study Bible, 2003 ed.

[2] *New Unger's Bible Dictionary,* PC Study Bible, 2003 ed.

[3] Dr. H. L. Willmington, *Willmington's Guide to the Bible* (Tyndale House Publishing, 1984) p. 66-67.

4 the shema, deuteronomy 6:4

*"**Hear, O Israel: The LORD our God is one LORD**: And thou shalt love the LORD thy God with all thine heart, and with all thy soul, and with all thy might. And these words, which I command thee this day, shall be in thine heart: And thou shalt teach them diligently unto thy children, and shalt talk of them when thou sittest in thine house, and when thou walkest by the way, and when thou liest down, and when thou risest up. And thou shalt bind them for a sign upon thine hand, and they shall be as frontlets between thine eyes. And thou shalt write them upon the posts of thy house, and on thy gates. And it shall be, when the LORD thy God shall have brought thee into the land which he sware unto thy fathers, to Abraham, to Isaac, and to Jacob, to give thee great and goodly cities, which thou buildedst not, And houses full of all good things, which thou filledst not, and wells digged, which thou diggedst not, vineyards and olive trees, which thou plantedst not; when thou shalt have eaten and be full; **Then beware lest thou forget the LORD**, which brought thee forth out of the land of Egypt, from the house of bondage. Thou shalt fear the LORD thy God, and serve him, and shalt swear by his name. Ye shall not go after other gods, of*

the gods of the people which are round about you;
(For the LORD thy God is a jealous God among
you) *lest the anger of the LORD thy God be kindled*
against thee, and destroy thee from off the face of the
earth. Ye shall not tempt the LORD your God, as ye
tempted him in Massah" (Deuteronomy 6:4-16).

When discussing doctrinal topics, especially on
the Godhead, it is amazing that two different people
can use the exact same verses of Scripture to provide
"proof" for two entirely different points of view. Yet
the Bible tells us that Scripture is not for *"private in-*
terpretation" (II Peter 1:21). To assist in deriving the
proper meaning from a text, there are certain standard principles of hermeneutics (the science and art
of Bible interpretation). The first and foremost is
that, in the simplest definition, Scripture means
what it says. Whenever possible, Scripture is to be
read with a literal interpretation in mind, taking into
account the context, background, and grammar of
the text. Unless indicated by the writer or the style of
the writing, Scripture is not to be allegorized. Simply
put, we shouldn't try to put meaning into a verse,
but rather we should try to get the meaning out of
the verse.

With that in mind, ***"Hear, O Israel: The LORD***
our God is one LORD" (Deuteronomy 6:4) means
God is One. How complicated is that? The Jews who
made this the cornerstone verse of their faith understood this to mean that God is numerically one. They
did not read into the verse meanings supported by
future theologians or future religious traditions. They
read what it said and properly concluded that God
meant what He said: He is One. Certainly this is con-

sistent with the revelation that Moses had previously received from God when He asked God what His name was. God responded, **"I AM That I AM"** *(Exodus 3:14).*

To the Hebrews, Deuteronomy 6:4 was called the *Shema,* which is the first word in this verse. *Shema* is the Hebrew word for "hear." Hear what? Hear that God is one. Unlike the pagans who inhabited the Promised Land and who worshipped multiple gods, the God of Israel was one in number. Throughout the pages of the Old Testament, when the children of Israel were not in a backslidden condition and were faithfully serving God, they vehemently contended for strict monotheism ("Mono" is of Greek derivation and means one; "theism" comes from the Greek root word for God). Without getting too far ahead of ourselves, that is exactly why the Jews rejected Jesus. They knew that Jesus was claiming to be the One God of Deuteronomy 6:4 and Exodus 3:14 and they just didn't understand how that could be possible.

The *Shema* further commanded the Hebrews to love the One God of Deuteronomy 6:4 and to teach their children about One God. They were to "advertise" their belief in One God by writing Deuteronomy 6:4 on the doorposts and gates of their homes and to bind them on their wristbands and foreheads before prayer. Why? They were to be constantly reminded that God was One. Even today orthodox Jews continue to follow these ancient practices.

The *Shema* was given to the children of Israel approximately one month before their entrance into the Promised Land. The entire Book of Deuteronomy is often referred to as the "Second Law." In it Moses was reviewing and underscoring the principles and commands of God with the generation that had not died in the Wilderness. They would be expected to carry on and abide by the faith of their fathers when they entered the Promised Land. Central to that faith was the belief in One God.

Thus the importance of the follow up commandment of Deuteronomy 6:12, "*Then beware lest thou forget the LORD.*" What LORD? The One LORD God of Deuteronomy 6:4. Not the triune god of a man's imagination. The **I AM That I AM** of Exodus 3:14. The Lord God confirmed that He was a jealous God in Deuteronomy 6:15 and would not share His glory with another. This verse makes it abundantly clear that if Israel deviated from the truth of One God, He would destroy them. True to His Word, when Israel would not repent from her backslidings and idolatrous practices, Israel was eventually led into Assyrian captivity and likewise Judah was led into Babylonian Captivity.

Most modern day Christians believe the Ceremonial Law of Moses is filled with archaic commands that have little relevance for us today. But those commands were written for our admonition. They were written with purpose and intent. Leviticus 19:19 reads, *"Ye shall keep my statutes. Thou shalt not let thy cattle gender with a diverse kind: thou shalt not sow thy field with mingled seed: neither shall a garment mingled of linen and woolen come upon thee."* Why? God's people were to be constantly reminded that He is One. The Philistines, Amorites, and Canaanites could sow different kinds of seeds in the same field much like we typically plant a variety of vegetables in our garden plots today. But the Israelites were forbidden to do so. The children of Israel were only allowed to plant one type of seed in a field. When the Israelite farmers went out to work in their fields, it was a visual object lesson to reaffirm their belief in the One True God. Likewise when they saw their pagan neighbor's fields sown with different kinds of seeds, the Israelites were reminded that they were not like them!

The children of Israel couldn't plow their fields with a mixed team. Again the message was clear: God is one. When an Israelite put on his garment in the morning, it was to be made of one fiber. It was another reminder that God is one. The Israelites couldn't mix linen and wool to have a blended fabric because it would lead to a false representation of God. The God of Israel was not two in one or three in one: He was one. The Laws of Leviticus 19:19 were another way for God to convey the message of Deuteronomy 6:13, **"Then beware lest thou forget the LORD."** National obedience to the ceremonial law was critical to the preservation of the doctrine of the One indivisible God of Israel.

Trinitarians argue that "one" does not mean numerical oneness in Deuteronomy 6:4. They suggest that "one" or *echad* in Hebrew means "one in unity." Although the Hebrew word *echad* can mean numerical oneness or one in unity[1], they choose the latter definition because it fits their traditional view of the Godhead. But an exhaustive search of the use of *echad* in the Old Testament reveals that this word is regularly used to show numerical oneness. Theologian, David Bernard writes:

"Biblical examples of the word used in the sense of absolute numerical oneness are enlightening:

a list of Canaanite kings each designated by the word "echad" (Joshua 12:9-24, the prophet Micaiah (I Kings 22:8); Abraham (Ezekiel 33:24; a list of gates each designated by "echad" (Ezekiel 48:31-34); and the angel Michael (Daniel 10:13). Certainly, in each of the above cases "echad" means one in numerical value."[2]

When *echad* is used to indicate unity, that is generally clear from the context. For example, the man and the woman became one or the people of Israel were one. In other words, the word is used to show the coming together of a plurality into a unified group. But the members of the group continue to be individual beings. The context makes this clear. But when it is used to describe an individual, it means numerical oneness. The Shema says Our God is one, not our Gods are one. God is not a group of individuals. We wouldn't say the people is one. We would say the people are one. God is one indicates that God is not a plural but a singular being.

In light of the hundreds of Old Testament verses representing God as one and the Old Testament's repetitive use of singular pronouns relative to God, it is clear that Deuteronomy 6:4 is speaking about God as one in number. Returning to an earlier thought, it is evident that some try to put meaning into a verse rather than taking the intended meaning out of the verse. In some cases this is the only way that they can "prove" a non-biblical doctrine.

It is absurd to surmise from Deuteronomy 6:4 that God did not mean He was numerically one as some trinitarians suggest. The Hebrews were God's chosen people. God worked and spoke through the Hebrew people as they became the depository for His

Truth. The Hebrews wrote the Old Testament and, for that matter, most of the New Testament! Hebrew was the language of the Old Testament. To think that the Hebrews themselves could not interpret or understand their own language and that it would take 2nd, 3rd, and 4th century philosophers and theologians, or modern day Christians, to tell the Hebrews what their own language was really saying in Deuteronomy 6:4 is arrogant at best, incredulous at least, and utterly preposterous. In fact, one of the primary reasons many Jews reject Christianity today is because of the totally foreign concept of a three in one god when their entire belief system is based upon the one God of Deuteronomy 6:4.

What separated the children of Israel from their pagan neighbors was not so much their style of worship as it was the object of their worship. The pagans offered blood sacrifices, practiced ritual washings, used censors and incense, had celebrated priesthoods attired in special apparel, and erected magnificent temples, not unlike the Israelites. But while the pagans worshiped multiple gods, the Israelites were commanded to worship One God.

Today some may view evangelical Christians as a single body of believers just going by different names. After all, they have similar ecclesiastical structures, worship services, and church buildings. But all evangelical Christians are not the same. The difference comes in the object of their worship. Some have opted for devotion to a triune god, while others have contended for the worship of the One True God of Deuteronomy 6:4. And in the end, that will make every difference.

[1] James Strong, *Strong's Exhaustive Concordance*, (Abingdon, 1890).

[2] David Bernard, *The Oneness of God*, (Word Aflame Press, 2000) p. 152-153.

5

isaiah's view of the godhead

Isaiah is often referred to as the Messianic Prophet because he so clearly saw the coming of Christ. The Book of Isaiah has been referred to as "The Gospel According to Isaiah" and some have even dubbed Isaiah the "Fifth Evangelist" or Gospel writer because of his keen foreknowledge of the coming Messiah. The most prominent phrase in the Book of Isaiah is the "Holy One of Israel" and is found 33 times. The Book of Isaiah has three divisions and each revolves around the central theme of the book, the Holy One of Israel. In chapters 1-35 the Holy One of Israel is rebuking and judging the nations, in chapters 36-39 the Holy One of Israel is delivering Hezekiah from his troubles, and in chapters 40-66 the Holy One of Israel is comforting and redeeming.[1]

How did Isaiah view the Godhead? First of all it must be remembered that Isaiah was a devout mono-theistic Jew. He wholeheartedly adhered to the *Shema, "Hear, O Israel: The LORD our God is one LORD" (Deuteronomy 6:4)*. Furthermore he fully embraced the teachings of the Ten Commandments. Commandments One and Two read:

"I am the LORD thy God, which have brought thee out of the land of Egypt, out of the house of bondage. **Thou shalt have no other gods before me***. Thou shalt not make unto thee any graven image, or any likeness of any thing that is in heaven above, or that is in the earth beneath, or that is in the water under the earth: Thou shalt not bow down thyself to them, nor serve them:* **for I the LORD thy God am a jealous God***, visiting the iniquity of the fathers upon the children unto the third and fourth generation of them that hate me; And shewing mercy unto thousands of them that love me, and keep my commandments" (Exodus 20:2-6).*

The Ten Commandments open with a powerful proclamation of God's absolute oneness. Note that Commandment One begins with the personal pronoun "I." No triune god here. Note also that Commandments One and Two are making an adamant prohibition against the worship of any other gods or images. Commandment Two adds the caveat that the One True God is a jealous God. The God of the Ten Commandments makes it clear that He will not share His glory with any other. How does that leave room for supposed second and third persons in the Godhead?

Now let's turn to Isaiah's own words to get his view on the Godhead. This is only a sampling of his writings, but the following quotes from the Book of Isaiah underscore his doctrinal belief in One God. Notice the pronouns in reference to God are always singular. Notice how often the phase "Holy One" is used and how many times God emphatically states that there is no one beside Him:

"To whom then will ye liken me, or shall I be equal? **saith the Holy One"** (Isaiah 40:25).

"Who hath wrought and done it, calling the generations from the beginning? **I the LORD, the first, and with the last; I am he**" (Isaiah 41:4).

"Fear thou not; for **I am with thee**: be not dismayed; for **I am thy God: I will strengthen thee;** yea, **I will help thee**; yea, **I will uphold thee** with the right hand of my righteousness" (Isaiah 41:10).

"**I am the LORD: that is my name: and my glory will I not give to another**, neither my praise to graven images" (Isaiah 42:8).

"Ye are my witnesses, saith the LORD, and my servant whom I have chosen: that ye may know and believe me, and understand that **I am he: before me there was no God formed, neither shall there be after me. I, even I, am the LORD; and beside me there is no saviour**. I have declared, and have saved, and I have shewed, when there was no strange god among you: therefore ye are my witnesses, saith the LORD, that **I am God**. Yea, before the day was **I am he**; and there is none that can deliver out of my hand: I will work, and who shall let it? **Thus saith the LORD, your redeemer, the Holy One of Israel;** For your sake I have sent to Babylon, and have brought down all their nobles, and the Chaldeans, whose cry is in the ships. **I am the LORD, your Holy One, the creator of Israel, your King**" (Isaiah 43:10-15).

*"**Thus saith the LORD the King of Israel, and his redeemer the LORD of hosts; I am the first, and I am the last; and beside me there is no God**" (Isaiah 44:6).*

*"Fear ye not, neither be afraid: have not I told thee from that time, and have declared it? ye are even my witnesses. **Is there a God beside me? yea, there is no God; I know not any**" (Isaiah 44:8).*

*"**I am the LORD, and there is none else, there is no God beside me**: I girded thee, though thou hast not known me" (Isaiah 45:5).*

*"Verily thou art a God that hidest thyself, **O God of Israel, the Saviour**" (Isaiah 45:15).*

*"For thus saith the LORD that created the heavens; God himself that formed the earth and made it; he hath established it, he created it not in vain, he formed it to be inhabited: **I am the LORD; and there is none else**" (Isaiah 45:18).*

*"Tell ye, and bring them near; yea, let them take counsel together: who hath declared this from ancient time? who hath told it from that time? have not I the LORD? and **there is no God beside me; a just God and a Saviour; there is none beside me**" (Isaiah 45:21).*

*"Remember the former things of old: **for I am God, and there is none else; I am God, and there is none like me**" (Isaiah 46:9).*

*"For mine own sake, even for mine own sake, will I do it: for how should my name be polluted? and **I will not give my glory unto another**. Hearken unto me, O Jacob and Israel, my called; **I am he; I am the first, I also am the last**"* (Isaiah 48:11-12).

Isaiah did not get a revelation of a triune god through his encounters with the LORD God of Israel. There is simply no allusion to a triune god in any of the above verses. God proclaims, through the Prophet Isaiah, that there is no God beside Him. Think about it. What is the prophet saying? What is God saying? There is no one beside Him, there is no one standing on His right hand, there is no one sitting on His right hand, there is no spirit like creature fluttering over Him like a dove. He alone is God and He knows no other. Those that add persons to the Godhead in essence are claiming to know more than God knows since God knows no other person in the Godhead (Isaiah 44:8).

Isaiah prophesied about the coming of the LORD God: *"The voice of him that crieth in the wilderness, Prepare ye the way of the **LORD**, make straight in the desert a highway for our **God**. Every valley shall be exalted, and every mountain and hill shall be made low: and the crooked shall be made straight, and the rough places plain: And the glory of the **LORD** shall be revealed, and all flesh shall see it together: for the mouth of the **LORD** hath spoken it"* (Isaiah 40:3-5).

According to Isaiah, John the Baptist's ministry was to prepare the way for the coming of the LORD God of Israel. That makes the LORD (Jehovah) God (Elohim) of Israel none other than Jesus Christ,

God manifested in flesh (I Timothy 3:16). When John the Baptist preached repentance (Matthew 3:1-3) and subsequently introduced Jesus as the Lamb of God who would take away the sins of the world (John 1:29), He fulfilled the prophecy of Isaiah 40:3. John the Baptist prepared the way of the LORD (Jehovah) and mankind beheld the glory of God (Elohim) in flesh. Whom did men behold? Jesus Christ, the express image of the invisible God of the Old Testament (Hebrews 1:3)!

The scene in the first chapter of the Gospel of John capturing John the Baptist's introduction of Jesus as the Messiah was one of immense incredulity for John the Baptist. Since Jesus and John were first cousins through their mothers' relationship as sisters, these two boys had been raised together, played together, and worked together. Although John the Baptist may have had a premonition that Jesus was a very special child and was destined for great things, he had no idea that Jesus was the Messiah. After all, he was thought to be the carpenter's son, not the Son of God. John the Baptist was truly astonished to learn by direct revelation from God that Jesus was the Messiah.

Only a few months later—his ministry completed—John the Baptist was set to be executed by Herod Antipas. While rotting in a filthy Roman prison and waiting for his beheading, John the Baptist let time and despair lead to fresh doubts about Jesus' identity. John, seeking some reassurance, especially since he was about to give his life for Him, asked two of his disciples to return to Jesus and ask Him if He really was the One for whom Israel had been waiting (Matthew 11:2-5). Jesus told the disciples to return to John and quote the following passage of Scripture from Isaiah 35:4-6:

*"Say to them that are of a fearful heart, Be strong, fear not: behold, your God will come with vengeance, even **God** with a recompence; **he will come and save you**. Then the eyes of the blind shall be opened, and the ears of the deaf shall be un-stopped. Then shall the lame man leap as an hart, and the tongue of the dumb sing: for in the wilderness shall waters break out, and streams in the desert."*

Jesus could just as easily have told the disciples to tell John the Baptist, "Yes, I Am the One." But Jesus chose rather to speak to John the Baptist through the prophet Isaiah. Using the words of Isaiah, Jesus reaffirmed that He was God (Elohim) and Savior. If John still had doubts, he need only look at the multiple miracles that Jesus had performed to assure him that Jesus was who He claimed to be. Nearly 700 years after his death, Isaiah was still testifying to another generation of prophets and the spiritually hungry that Jesus was God manifested in flesh!

One of the most quoted verses of Scripture in the Bible, especially at Christmas time, is Isaiah 9:6. If one had any doubts as to how Isaiah viewed Jesus, one would only have to read Isaiah 9:6: *"For unto us a child is born, unto us a son is given: and the government shall be upon his shoulder: and his name shall be called Wonderful, Counselor, the mighty God, the **everlasting Father**, the Prince of Peace."* Isaiah identified the coming Son as the everlasting Father! Why? For two reasons. First, Isaiah was inspired by

43

God to write Isaiah 9:6; second, it identified the coming Son as the Father Incarnate. Jesus wasn't the second person of the Godhead; He was the everlasting Father manifested in flesh (I Timothy 3:16).

There are 3 verses of Scripture in Isaiah that some use to support the false notion of a triune god: Isaiah 6:8, 48:16, and 63:9-10. These verses are singled out while ignoring the hundreds of singular references to God found throughout the Book of Isaiah.

In Isaiah 6:8 the *"who will go for us"* most likely refers to the angels or the righteous servants of God[2], not a triune god. Isaiah 48:16 uses the expression, *"the LORD God and his Spirit."* If this is an indication of multiple persons in the Godhead as some suggest, are we to assume then that the LORD God can be separated from his Spirit? God is a Spirit (John 4:24). How do you separate God from what He is? If Isaiah 48:16 raises a doubt in your mind about God's absolute oneness, you only have to read the next verse in the chapter to clear up the matter. Isaiah 48:17 proclaims, *"Thus saith the LORD, thy Redeemer, **the Holy One of Israel; I am the LORD thy God** which teacheth thee to profit, which leadeth thee by the way that thou shouldest go."*

Isaiah 63:9-10 also makes a reference to the LORD and his Spirit. Again, can God be separated from his own Spirit? Isaiah 63:14 answers the question with an emphatic "No!" Isaiah 63:14 reads, *"As a beast goeth down into the valley, **the Spirit of the LORD** caused him to rest: so didst thou lead thy people, to make thyself a glorious name."* The Spirit of the LORD is the singular Spirit of one God, not the third person in a threesome.

Carl Brumback, author of the book *God in Three Persons*, concurs that you cannot find a triune god in the Old Testament if you don't already have a preconceived idea of a triune god before you open its pages. He states, "If the New Testament did not exist we could not derive the doctrine of the trinity from the Old Testament."[3] Isaiah would agree!

Theologian and author Frank Tamel reports the following account: Some years ago a devout monotheistic Jew confessed that he and others of his faith were not convinced that Messiah was actually a person. Their theory of Messiah suggested that man, through education and enlightenment, would rise to the point where they would eliminate all wars, sickness, poverty and bigotry. At the fulfillment of these social reforms, it would be said, "Messiah has come." This committed Jew was then asked to read Isaiah 62:11: *"Behold, the LORD hath proclaimed unto the end of the world, Say ye to the daughter of Zion, **Behold, thy salvation cometh**; behold, **his** reward is with **him**, and his work before **him**."* Notice that Isaiah made it very clear in this verse that salvation was coming through a person as evidenced by the pronouns "his, him, and him."

This Jewish scholar was then asked to translate the English word "salvation" in this verse into Hebrew. He responded, "It is Yehsuha." Being equally conversant with the Greek language, he was then asked to translate "Yehsuha" into Greek. Knowing that he had unwittingly trapped himself, he begrudgingly acknowledged, "The Hebrew word 'Yeshua' is translated 'Jesus' in the Greek." He had just stumbled upon the great truth of the Book of Isaiah: Jesus is God!

[1] Robert Lee, *The Outlined Bible* (Zondervan Publishing House, 1981), p. 23.
[2] Bernard, p. 152.
[3] Carl Brumback, *God in Three Persons* (Pathway Press, 1959), p. 54.

6 what is god's name?

Throughout the Old Testament the One God of Israel distanced and distinguished Himself from the multiple deities of the heathen nations that surrounded Israel. The God of Israel was invisible (Hebrews 11:27, Colossians 1:15). The God of Israel refused to be downgraded to the status of an icon (Exodus 20:4-5). The God of Israel declared that He was the only God (Deuteronomy 6:4). The God of Israel revealed Himself through Creation, by signs and wonders, and as previously discussed in Chapter 2, through His names and titles. But to the Old Testament saints there was an understanding that God had a Name that was above every other name and that it had yet to be revealed: *And the LORD shall be king over all the earth: in that day shall there be **one** LORD, and **his name one**" (Zechariah 14:9).* The Patriarchs, the Lawgiver, the Prophets, and common Israelite citizens longed for the mystery name of God to be revealed.

To the ancients of Bible times names were especially significant. Names were chosen because they meant something, signified a truth, expressed a person's destiny, or captured one's personality or nature.[1] For instance Samuel means "asked of God," as he was an answer to Hannah's prayer for a child. Isaiah's name reflected his Messianic Message, "Jehovah Saves." God often chose to change the names of His servants to more accurately express their destiny. Thus Abram (exalted father) became Abraham: the father of a great multitude. When God changed Abraham's name He also changed Abraham's wife's name from Sarai (contentious) to Sarah (princess) to better reflect her future status as the mother of a nation.

Pagan rulers understood this principle as well. Upon Joseph's interpretation of Pharaoh's dream, Pharaoh renamed Joseph, Zaphnathpaaneah (Genesis 41:45). Zaphnathpaaneah was the Egyptian equivalent of "savior of the world[2]." Pharaoh understood that God had sent Joseph to preserve or "save" Egypt from the devastating affects of the upcoming seven-year famine and thus named him accordingly.

The Babylonians purposely changed Daniel's name (Judge of Jehovah) to Belteshazzar (Baal protect his life) in an attempt to get the exiled Jew to forget the God of his fathers. The same can be said of the 3 Hebrew Children. Hananiah (the LORD is Gracious) became known as Shadrach (lover of Baal), Mishael (who is like our God) became known as Meshach (bow to Baal), and Azariah (the LORD is my Keeper) became known as Abednego (servant of Nebo). Thank God that these men lived up to their Hebrew names and did not submit to their Babylonian names! Ironically, today's Christian community is more likely to identify the 3 Hebrew Children by their Babylonian names rather than by their Hebrew names. Where Nebuchadnezzar failed, we have regrettably "succeeded."

It seems obvious then, if not even trite, to state that if the names of mortal men hold such significance in the Bible, how much more significant is the Name of God as revealed in the pages of Scripture? Which brings us back to the original question, "What is God's Name?"

I have asked hundreds of people, most professing Christians, this very question. The answers are as varied as they are astounding. Some suggests God's Name is God! When asked how that "name" distinguishes the Christian God from any other deity, I usually get a blank or quizzical expression. Some suggest His Name is Father, Jehovah, Yahweh, or El Shaddai. I have heard Christians sing with full throttled passion, "Jehovah is His Name." Is Jehovah really His Name? Is God or Father His Name? Is El-Shaddai His Name?

Five Old Testament Inquiries Asking After God's Name[3]

From the beginning of time, man has longed to know God and to know God's Name. The Patriarch Job was exasperated when his search for God appeared futile: *"Behold, I go forward, but he is not there; and backward, but I cannot perceive him: On the left hand, where he doth work, but I cannot behold him: he hideth himself on the right hand, that I cannot see him:" (Job 23:8-9).* Other Old Testament saints had a similar desire to know God and His Name.

Jacob had one such experience.

Jacob's Inquiry

"And Jacob was left alone; and there wrestled a man with him until the breaking of the day. And when

*he saw that he prevailed not against him, he touched the hollow of his thigh; and the hollow of Jacob's thigh was out of joint, as he wrestled with him. And he said, Let me go, for the day breaketh. And he said, I will not let thee go, except thou bless me. And he said unto him, What is thy name? And he said, Jacob. And he said, Thy name shall be called no more Jacob, but Israel: for as a prince hast thou power with God and with men, and hast prevailed. And Jacob asked him, and said, **Tell me, I pray thee, thy name.** And he said, **Wherefore is it that thou dost ask after my name?** And he blessed him there. And Jacob called the name of the place Peniel: for I have seen God face to face, and my life is preserved" (Genesis 32:24-30).*

Jacob's name means supplanter or deceitful one. Especially in the early years of his life, Jacob fully lived up to his name. What an indictment! Jacob cheated his brother, Esau, out of his birthright and the covenant blessing. For this, Esau hated him and vowed to kill him. Isaac exiled Jacob to Padan Aram ostensibly to find a wife, but also to escape the wrath of Esau. But Esau's prowess as an accomplished hunter was legendary and his carnal appetite to take what he wanted did not bode well for Jacob. Esau was prepared to hunt Jacob down like an animal, so great was his anger.

While in Padan Aram, Jacob the trickster was tricked over and over again by his uncle, Laban. After 21 years of service to Laban, Jacob had enough and set out to return home with his two wives, two handmaidens, eleven sons, and one daughter. As Jacob approached his homeland, he sent gifts ahead to Esau hoping to assuage the anger of his brother.

Jacob, who had depended on his wits and the arm of flesh for most of his life, now realized that the gifts might not be enough to appease Esau. This led to Jacob's Jabok River prayer meeting as recorded in Genesis 32:24-30.

It is interesting to note that once Jacob got the answer to his prayer—namely, the promise of his family's preservation—it wasn't enough to satisfy him. Once in the presence of God, Jacob wanted to know God. He wanted to know God's Name. When he asked the Angel of the LORD for his Name, the response was essentially, "You got what you came here for, but you are not going to know Me by My Name." Thus the famous wrestling match ended without Jacob receiving the revelation of God's Name.

Jacob's question may seem curious at first. After all why would he ask after God's Name when God had already revealed Himself as God, El-Shaddai, Adonai, and Jehovah-Jireh? The answer is simple. The children of Abraham knew and understood that God wasn't God's name. Nor was El-Shaddai, Adonai, or Jehovah. They were titles, descriptions; but not THE name. Jacob inquired after the mystery Name of God but was left without an answer.

Moses' Inquiry

As discussed in Chapter 3, Moses inquired after God's Name when God met with him at the burning bush: *"And God said unto Moses, I AM THAT I AM: and he said, Thus shalt thou say unto the children of Israel, I AM hath sent me unto you" (Exodus 3:14).* The language is unambiguous. God is an "I AM," not a "WE ARE." But everyone would have to agree that, "I AM THAT I AM" is not a name. It is a combination of two singular pronouns reiterating God's absolute Oneness and proclaiming Him as the Self Existent One. Moses was not satisfied with the answer. Like Jacob before him, Moses longed to hear the Name of God. Moses equally understood that God's name was not God, El-Shaddai, Adonai, Jehovah-Jireh, or even I AM THAT I AM.

In His mercy, God again spoke to Moses and drew the curtain of revelation back a bit further: *"And God spake unto Moses, and said unto him, I am the LORD: And I appeared unto Abraham, unto Isaac, and unto Jacob, by the name of God Almighty, but by my name JEHOVAH was I not known to them" (Exodus 6:2-3).* It is true that Abraham knew God as God Almighty (El-Shaddai) and as Jehovah-Jireh (God Provides), but Abraham did not link the Name of Jehovah with salvation. God now revealed to Moses that His Name would convey the message of salvation and redemption.

But Jehovah is not the final and full revelation of God's Name!

Manoah's Inquiry

If Jehovah is God's Name as some suggest, then Manoah did not have to ask God the question, "What is your name?" because the name Jehovah had already been passed down to him through Moses. Judges 13:16-17 reads, *"And Manoah said unto the angel of the LORD, What is thy name, that when thy sayings come to pass we may do thee honour? And the angel of the LORD said unto him, Why askest thou thus after my name, seeing it is secret?"*

God put Manoah on notice that His Name was still a secret and that the hour of its revelation had not yet come.

Judges 13:19-22 makes it clear that Manoah was indeed conversing with the LORD: *"So Manoah took a kid with a meat offering, and offered it upon a rock unto the LORD: and the angel did wondrously; and Manoah and his wife looked on. For it came to pass, when the flame went up toward heaven from off the altar, that the angel of the LORD ascended in the flame of the altar. And Manoah and his wife looked on it, and fell on their faces to the ground. But the angel of the LORD did no more appear to Manoah and to his wife. Then Manoah knew that he was an angel of the LORD. And Manoah said unto his wife, We shall surely die, because **we have seen God**."*

Like his Hebrew predecessors, Manoah was waiting for God to reveal His mystery Name. Although Manoah was blessed with a son, he was not allowed to know the mystery Name of God.

Agur's Inquiry

The Prophet Agur repeats the Old Testament mantra: *"Who hath ascended up into heaven, or descended? who hath gathered the wind in his fists? who hath bound the waters in a garment? who hath established all the ends of the earth? **what is his name, and what is his son's name, if thou canst tell**"* (Proverbs 30:4). Even the prophets with all their spiritual insight could not unravel the mystery of God's hidden Name. Solomon, renowned for his wisdom, author of over 3,000 proverbs and 1,000 songs, and a contemporary of Agur, could not answer the question, "What is His Name?"

Agur does have a prophetic glimpse. He sees the God of the Old Testament coming as the Son, and like so many before him, wonders after His Name. "But his anointing could not reveal what God had chosen to conceal."[4]

Isaiah's Inquiry

As discussed in Chapter Five, Isaiah had an insatiable appetite to know God and to know God's Name. His quest was not diminished when he saw "the LORD high and lifted up" in Isaiah 6. In Isaiah 7:14, the prophet proclaims, *"Therefore the Lord himself shall give you a sign; Behold, a virgin shall conceive, and bear a son, and* **shall call his name Immanuel.***"* He also further revealed the following information about the son: *"For unto us a child is born, unto us a son is given: and the government shall be upon his shoulder: and his name shall be called Wonderful, Counsellor, The mighty God, The everlasting Father, The Prince of Peace"* (Isaiah 9:6). Isaiah foretold that the Son would be "Immanuel" or "God with us" and that the Son would be none other than the "Everlasting Father."

The monotheistic Jews never anticipated that when Shiloh or Messiah finally came, He would be any one other than God Himself. In a prophetic sense, Isaiah and Agur underscored the point that God would come in flesh as the Son. Isaiah concluded that "Immanuel" is not the secret Name of God, but rather a revelation that God the Father will be with us in flesh. Immanuel would come from the lineage of David (Isaiah 11:1) and would be born of a virgin (Isaiah 7:14). Then the clincher, Isaiah positively identifies the coming Son as the Everlasting Father and the Mighty God (Isaiah 9:6)!

Revelation of the Mystery Name of God

Note how the writer of the Book of Hebrews summed up the Old Testament era. After testifying to the exploits of the Old Testament greats in what is often referred to as the "Hall of Faith," the writer returns to the central theme of the Old Testament—expectation and longing for the coming of Messiah and the subsequent disappointment of the Old Testament faithful as they all died in faith having not received the promise of God:

"These all died in faith, not having received the promises, but having seen them afar off, and were persuaded of them, and embraced them, and confessed that they were strangers and pilgrims on the earth. And these all, having obtained a good report through faith, received not the promise:" (Hebrews 11:13, 39).

What promise did these faithful men and women of God not receive? The Old Testament faithful died without ever hearing the mystery Name of God, without ever having a full understanding of the revelation of the Mighty God in Christ.

But in the New Testament, the mystery Name of God is at long last revealed. The Apostle Paul explains the revelation of the mystery Name of God like this, *"But when the fulness of the time was come, God* sent forth his Son, made of a woman, made under the law" (Galatians 4:4). The mystery Name of God would come through the birth of the Son of God!

The first to hear the mystery Name of God was the angel Gabriel when he was dispatched by God to deliver the Name to Mary and Joseph. The second people to hear the mystery Name of God were Mary and Joseph:

"And in the sixth month the **angel Gabriel** was sent from God unto a city of Galilee, named Nazareth, To a virgin espoused to a man whose name was Joseph, of the house of David; and the virgin's name was Mary. And the angel came in unto her, and said, Hail, thou that art highly favoured, the Lord is with thee: blessed art thou among women. And when she saw him, she was troubled at his saying, and cast in her mind what manner of salutation this should be. And the angel said unto her, Fear not, Mary: for thou hast found favour with God. And, behold, thou shalt conceive in thy womb, and bring forth a son, and **shalt call his name JESUS**. He shall be great, and shall be called the Son of the Highest: and the Lord God shall give unto him the throne of his father David: And he shall reign over the house of Jacob for ever; and of his kingdom there shall be no end. Then said Mary unto the angel, How shall this be, seeing I know not a man? And the angel answered and said unto her, The Holy Ghost shall come upon thee, and the power of the Highest shall overshadow thee: therefore also that holy thing which shall be born of thee shall be called the Son of God" (Luke 1:26-35).

Gabriel had at long last communicated the message that God's people had longed to hear when he instructed Mary to name her baby **JESUS**. When Joseph was suspect at best over Mary's explanation of her pregnancy, Gabriel reiterated the mystery Name of God to him:

"Now the birth of Jesus Christ was on this wise: When as his mother Mary was espoused to Joseph, before they came together, she was found with child of the Holy Ghost. Then Joseph her husband, being a just man, and not willing to make her a publick example, was minded to put her away privily. But while he thought on these things, behold, the angel of the Lord appeared unto him in a dream, saying, Joseph, thou son of David, fear not to take unto thee Mary thy wife: for that which is conceived in her is of the Holy Ghost. And she shall bring forth a son, and **thou shalt call his name JESUS***: for* **he shall save his people from their sins***. Now all this was done, that it might be fulfilled which was spoken of the Lord by the prophet, saying, Behold, a virgin shall be with child, and shall bring forth a son, and they* **shall call his name Emmanuel***, which being interpreted is,* **God with us***. Then Joseph being raised from sleep did as the angel of the Lord had bidden him, and took unto him his wife: And knew her not till she had brought forth her firstborn son: and* **he called his name JE-SUS***" (Matthew 1:18-25).*

Note the message Gabriel delivered. **The child** to be born **would be God with us!** The promised child was not the second member of a supposed triune Godhead; He was the manifestation of the invisible God of the Old Testament (Colossians 1:15, He-brews 1:3). The Apostle Paul proclaimed, *"And with-out controversy great is the mystery of godliness:* **God was manifest in the flesh**, *justified in the Spirit, seen of angels, preached unto the Gentiles, believed on in the world, received up into glory" (I Timothy 3:16).*

The shepherds were next in line to hear the good news. *"And there were in the same country shepherds abiding in the field, keeping watch over their flock by night. And, lo, the angel of the Lord came upon them, and the glory of the Lord shone round about them: and they were sore afraid. And the angel said unto them, Fear not: for, behold, I bring you good tidings of great joy, which shall be to all people.* **For unto you is born this day in the city of David a Saviour, which is Christ the Lord***" (Luke 2:8-11).*

Jehovah, or God the Father, had already pro-claimed that He was the only Savior: *"I, even I, am the LORD; and beside me there is no saviour" (Isaiah 43:11).* The only way that Jesus could be the Savior was to be the Incarnation of the Old Testament God of Israel.

The Temple elders were next to hear the mys-tery name of God: *"And when eight days were ac-complished for the circumcising of the child,* **his name was called JESUS**, *which was so named of the angel before he was conceived in the womb" (Luke 2:21).*

At the revelation of the Name of Jesus, angels praised (Luke 2:13-14) and shepherds praised and glorified (Luke 2:21). Simeon proclaimed that he had finally seen the *"consolation of Israel"* (Luke 2:25) and his *"salvation"* (Luke 2:30). Likewise, when Anna the prophetess saw Jesus in the Temple at the time of his circumcision, she acknowledged her *"redemption"* (Luke 2:38).

The mystery Name had at long last been revealed. Luke allowed that Jesus was the one and only Name that could provide for salvation (Acts 4:12). Why? Because in the Apostle Paul's words, *"For in him dwelleth all the fullness of the Godhead bodily" (Colossians 2:9).* Jesus was not just a "chip off the old block;" He was the Block manifested in flesh! The Bible says that Jesus came in His Father's Name (John 5:43). That makes the Father's Name Jesus! This was the answer to the Prophet Agur's question. Jesus is the Name of the Father and the Son!

The Gospel writer John could not have been any clearer: *"In the beginning was the Word, and the Word was with God, and the Word was God (John 1:1). And the Word was made flesh, and dwelt among us, (and we beheld his glory, the glory as of the only begotten of the Father,) full of grace and truth" (John 1:14).* You cannot separate God from His Word. The Word is God. And the Word became flesh. Who became flesh? The God of the Old Testament became flesh. Jesus is the glory of the Father, because He is the Incarnation of the Word, the Incarnation of the Father.

As noted throughout this chapter, the Old Testament saints longed for the mystery Name of God to be revealed. Notice that once the Name of Jesus is made known to God's people, there is only one other recorded instance in the Bible where a Jew asks after God's Name. In Acts 9, Saul of Tarsus (a devout, monotheistic, *"Hear, O Israel: The LORD our God is one LORD:" (Deuteronomy 6:4).* Jew) asks after the mystery Name of God when he was struck down on the road to Damascus. Saul cried out, *"Who art thou, Lord?* **And the Lord said, I am Jesus** *whom thou persecutest: it is hard for thee to kick against the pricks" (Acts 9:5).* God answered Saul in the only way He could, **"I AM JESUS!"** Saul received the revelation of the Mighty God in Christ! Have you?

---

[1] Bernard, pp. 42-43.

[2] *Fausset's Bible Dictionary*, PC Study Bible, 2003 ed.

[3] T. B. Neil, *Understanding the Godhead,* (Page Master Publication Services Inc. 2002), pp. 2-6.

[4] Ibid., p. 4.

7 who is jesus?

If the answer to the previous chapter's question, "What is God's Name?" is Jesus, then it follows that Jesus is God. Jesus is God manifested in flesh (I Timothy 3:16). Jesus is the express image of the invisible God (Colossians 1:15, Hebrews 1:3). Jesus is not the second person of a triune Godhead; He is the Incarnation of the One True God!

The key to understanding the Godhead is to understand that Jesus Christ was both Man and God. He was the son of Mary and she conceived by the overshadowing of the Holy Ghost (Matthew 1:18). That is why Jesus was referred to as both Son of Man and Son of God. Humanity and divinity united in Christ for the purpose of salvation. The Bible says, *"To wit, that* **God was in Christ**, **reconciling the world unto himself**, *not imputing their trespasses unto them; and hath committed unto us the word of reconciliation" (2 Corinthians 5:19).* Which God was in Christ? The God of the Old Testament. The God of Deuteronomy 6:4.

The Purpose of the Incarnation

Fallen man could not be saved without a Savior. Although the children of Israel made atonement for their sins through animal sacrifices, these sacrifices could not wash away their sins. At best they could push their sins ahead for another year in anticipation of the coming Savior. Animal blood is inferior to human blood, so animal blood could never wash away man's sin.

The best of mortal men—Abraham, Moses, Elijah, Isaiah, and Daniel immediately come to mind—even had they been willing to do so, could not have offered their lives as a sacrifice for mankind's sins because, *"All have sinned and come short of the glory of God" (Romans 3:23).* John the Baptist, of whom it was said, *"Among those that are born of women there is not a greater prophet than John the Baptist" (Luke 7:28)* could not relieve man of the burden of his sins through the message of repentance. At his own admission John the Baptist stated, *"I indeed baptize you with water unto repentance: but he that cometh after me is mightier than I, whose shoes I am not worthy to bear: he shall baptize you with the Holy Ghost, and with fire:" (Matthew 3:11).*

When John the Baptist saw Jesus coming in John 1:29, his eyes were opened by God and he beheld the Savior of the world, saying, *"The next day John seeth Jesus coming unto him, and saith, Behold the Lamb of God, which taketh away the sin of the world."* While they were growing up together, John may have had some peculiar notion that Jesus was someone special, but he had no idea that Jesus was the Savior until it was revealed to him by God. When the revelation came, however, John immediately understood that Jesus was the Lamb of God or the flesh of God, the long-awaited Messiah, the One that would be the sacrifice for fallen man's sins. When John's faith faltered concerning the true identity of his cousin, Jesus confirmed His identity by proclaiming He was the fulfillment of Isaiah 35:3-6, the God of the Old Testament coming as the Healer and Savior. (Chapter Five has a more complete explanation of this passage.)

God is a Spirit (John 4:24). A Spirit does not have flesh and bones (Luke 24:39). God's plan, even before the foundation of the world (Ephesians 1:4, I Peter 1:20) was that He would put on flesh for the purpose of Redemption. Since without the shedding of blood there is no remission of sins (Hebrews 9:22) and since animal and mere human blood are not efficacious in the washing away of man's sin, God became flesh (I Timothy 3:16) so He could go to the Cross, shed innocent blood, and make provision for the remission of a man's sins: *"Forasmuch as ye know that ye were not redeemed with corruptible things, as silver and gold, from your vain conversation received by tradition from your fathers; But with the precious blood of Christ, as of a lamb without blemish and without spot:" (I Peter 1:18-19).*

God had to come in flesh for the purpose of Redemption. What God chose not to accomplish in the Spirit realm, He accomplished through His own Incarnation. The thought that He would send a second person to do the "dirty work" of Redemption is blasphemous, insulting, and denigrates the integrity of God. What kind of a "loving" God expresses His love to mankind by sending someone else to get abused and killed on our behalf? It's absurd. It is certainly not the picture of a loving God, much less a loving Father.

Jesus Is Both God and Man

Too many of today's professing Christians are saddled with a so-called orthodox definition of the Godhead which was manufactured by Greek philosophers masquerading as theologians centuries after the Day of Pentecost and the birth of the Church. No wonder there is such confusion over Christ's identity. Jesus said, *"And if the blind lead the blind, both shall fall into the ditch" (Matthew 15:14).*

It is misleading and erroneous to suggest that Jesus is any one other than God manifest in flesh. The divine mystery of the Incarnation is incomprehensible to man in the sense that the human mind cannot comprehend how an invisible God could become a man. But the Incarnation is not incomprehensible in the sense that God did become a man. He has told us that He became a man (I Timothy 3:16) and that should settle it.

Jesus Christ was both man and God. Jesus had two natures. As a man he was born of a woman (Luke 2:7). Like any other man, he got hungry (Matthew 4:2), thirsty (Luke 2:52), and tired (John 4:6). He grew in wisdom and stature (Luke 2:52). He prayed (Luke 22:41), became the sacrifice for our sins (Hebrews 10:10-12), and acknowledged that his Father was greater than he was (John 14:28). But as God, He is eternal (John 1:1-2). As God, He could multiply the fishes and loaves and feed the multitudes (Matthew 14:19-20). As God, He was Living Water (John 4:14) and as God He calmed the sea (Mark 4:39-41). As God, He answered prayer (John 14:14), and as God He forgave sin (Mark 2:5-7). As God, He knew no equal (John 5:18) and had all power (Matthew 28:18). As God, Jesus was the manifestation of the Father (John 10:30, 14:9).

There is not a distinction in persons in the Godhead, but there is a distinction between the humanity and divinity of Jesus. Once this is understood, so called "confusing verses" are more easily comprehended. When reading verses that seem to convey the thought of multiple persons in the Godhead, one must ask, is Jesus speaking as a man, as God, or both?

In his book *The Oneness of God,* David Bernard explains it this way.

"We must always remember that Jesus is fully God and not merely an anointed man. At the same time, He was fully human, not having just an appearance of humanity. He had a dual nature unlike anything we have, and we cannot adequately compare our existence or experience to His. What would seem strange or impossible if applied to a mere human becomes understandable when viewed in the context of One who is both fully God and fully human at the same time."[1]

Jesus Is the Incarnation of the Father

Jesus said, *"I and my Father are one" (John 10:30).* The wording of this verse couldn't be any more direct or emphatic. Jesus was asserting that He was the Father manifested in flesh. Some would suggest that this verse expresses unity rather than numeric oneness. If this were true, however, how can this verse be reconciled with John 14:8-9 which reads, *"Philip saith unto him, **Lord, shew us the Fa-***

ther, and it sufficeth us. **Jesus saith** *unto him, Have I been so long time with you, and yet hast thou not known me, Philip?* **he that hath seen me hath seen the Father; and how sayest thou then, Shew us the Father?**" Jesus was aghast that Philip, who had been with Jesus nearly from the beginning of His ministry, still did not know who He was. Jesus questioned Philip, how is it even possible that you don't know who I am? To help convince Philip of His identity, Jesus implored, *"Believest thou not that I am in the Father, and the Father in me? the words that I speak unto you I speak not of myself: but the Father that dwelleth in me, he doeth the works. Believe me that I am in the Father, and the Father in me: or else believe me for the very works' sake" (John 14:10-11).* Jesus prodded Philip: understand that I am in the Father and the Father is in me. On what basis was Philip to believe this assertion? On the basis of the miracles he had witnessed and the teachings he had heard.

Hear again the words of the Prophet Isaiah: *"For unto us* **a child is born,** *unto us* **a son is given***: and the government shall be upon his shoulder: and* **his name shall be called** *Wonderful, Counsellor, The mighty God,* **The everlasting Father,** *The Prince of Peace" (Isaiah 9:6).* Isaiah identified the son of Isaiah 7:14 as Immanuel or God with us. The birth of Jesus signaled God's willingness to live in a human body so that He could be "God with us" in a way that He could never have been with us in Spirit. Isaiah reconfirmed Jesus' identity by proclaiming that the "son" (the "God with us" of Isaiah 7:14) is the Incarnation of the Everlasting Father. Jesus was exhorting Philip: I am the visible representation of the invisible Father. I am God with you. I am the Incarnation of the Everlasting Father.

Jesus continued His Godhead lesson with Philip:

*"If ye shall ask any thing in my name, I will do it. If ye love me, keep my commandments. **And I will pray the Father, and he shall give you another Comforter**, that he may abide with you for ever; **Even the Spirit of truth; whom the world cannot receive, because it seeth him not, neither knoweth him: but ye know him; for he dwelleth with you,** and shall be in you. **I will not leave you comfortless**: I will come to you. Yet a little while, and the world seeth me no more; but ye see me: because I live, ye shall live also. At that day ye shall know that I am in my Father, and ye in me, and I in you" (John 14:14-20).*

Jesus was letting Philip know that He was also the Comforter or Holy Ghost. He told Philip that He would not leave him comfortless. Jesus claimed to be the Incarnation of the invisible Holy Spirit of God. Jesus prophesied to Philip that He would come again onto him through the infilling of the Holy Ghost. This was fulfilled in Acts 2:1-4 as Philip was among the 120 in the Upper Room on the Day of Pentecost (Acts 1:13). Jesus was essentially telling Philip that, "Although I cannot indwell you as a man, I will indwell you with My Spirit, the Holy Ghost, after My resurrection and ascension." His assurance to Philip was that as Philip gazed into the eyes of Jesus, he was actually looking at the Incarnation of the Holy Ghost. Jesus said as much. "In a little while the world will no longer be able to fasten their eyes upon the Spirit of Truth, but you, Philip, are looking at the Spirit of Truth right now." What was Philip looking at? He was looking at Jesus, the bodily image of the Spirit of Truth. The world in a short time would no longer be able to look at the Spirit of Truth because Jesus knew He would be crucified, die, and be buried. He would leave this world as a man, but would return as the Holy Ghost or Comforter to whosoever would receive Him. When a Christian is filled with the Holy Ghost or Holy Spirit, they have the Spirit of Christ in them (Colossians 1:27). That makes Jesus the Incarnation of the Holy Ghost.

Vine's Expository Dictionary of New Testament Words renders "comfortless" as "fatherless" in John 14². Jesus was freely interchanging the titles Father and Holy Ghost or Comforter. How could He do this? The Father is a Spirit. He is Holy. That makes the Father the Holy Spirit. The Father and Spirit are one in the same. You cannot separate the Father from His Spirit. Father speaks of God's relationship with man, but that does not negate His nature. God is a Spirit. The title Holy Spirit or Holy Ghost references God in action. But even when God is in action, He does not cease to be our Father.

Jesus never talked in terms of trinitarian dogma to Philip. Jesus told Philip in John 14, I am the Incarnation of the Father and the Holy Ghost. When you see Me, Philip, you are looking at the visible representation of the invisible Father, the invisible Holy Spirit of God. Although God condescended to take on a human form, Jesus did not cease to have all power. He did not cease to be the Father or the Holy Ghost: *"For in him dwelleth all the fulness of the Godhead bodily"* *(Colossians 2:9).* When God took on flesh, He became a man in the fullest sense. He was confined to location, time, and human frailty— something He had never done before. Yet He never ceased to be the omnipresent Spirit of God, the Father of all Creation.

[1] Bernard, p. 88
[2] *Vine's Expository Dictionary of New Testament Words,* (Flemming H. Revel, 1940).

8 the divine riddle

A collaboration of Christian scholars prepared the following definition of the Trinity doctrine in a pamphlet entitled "What Is the Trinity and What Do Christians Believe?":

"There is only one God, and this one God is in three Persons. The three Persons are God the Father, God the Son (Jesus Christ), and God the Holy Spirit (also called the Holy Ghost). The Persons are distinct: the Father is not the Son, the Son is not the Holy Spirit and the Holy Spirit is not the Father. God is one absolutely perfect divine Being in three Persons. The three are called Persons because they relate to one another in personal ways. The Father is God – the first person of the Trinity. The Son is God – the second Person of the Trinity. The Holy Spirit is God – the third Person of the Trinity."[1]

C. C. Ryrie adds, *"There is only one God, but in the unity of the Godhead there are three eternal and coequal Persons, the same in Substance, but distinct in subsistence."*[2]

Finis Dake defines the doctrine of the Trinity to include the following: *"There are three separate and distinct persons in the Godhead, each one having His own personal spirit body, personal soul, and personal spirit.."3*

The teaching of the Trinity also embodies the concept that God the Father, God the Son, and God the Holy Spirit are coequal, coeternal, and consubstantial. The Son is eternally begotten and is identified as the Word.

Really? Please reread these definitions. Are they logical? Are they sensible? Are they reasonable? Are they Biblical? The answer to all four questions is a resounding NO! First and foremost, how can God be relegated to "person" status? Is God a Person or Persons? Or is He God? How can one God exist as three Persons—each Person having his own separate spirit, soul, and body and each having a relationship with the other two members of the so-called trinity— yet still be one God?

By definition, trinitarians claim that the Father is not the Son, the Son is not the Holy Spirit, and the Holy Spirit is not the Father. Okay, then if the members of the trinity are separate and distinct persons, and one member is not the other member, it sure sounds like three to me. What kind of mathematics does it take to get $1 + 1 + 1 = 1$? Even a child knows that $1 + 1 + 1 = 3$. The trinitarian will argue that the mathematical equation for God is $1 \times 1 \times 1 = 1$.[4] Nice try, but this is a monumental deviation from the definition of the trinity. By definition, the three persons of the triune Godhead are one in unity, but not one in person. The three persons are specifically identified as the First Person, God the Father; the

Second Person, God the Son; and the Third Person, God the Holy Ghost.

Logic and reason would seemingly lead to a belief in One God. Apparently I'm not the only one that feels that way. Ward Williams writes the following in *The Pentecostal Evangel: "The reasons we reject modal monarchianism (Oneness) are not based on reason. In fact, reason would more readily accept the idea of one God manifested in three ways."*[5] (*The Pentecostal Evangel* is the official organ of the Assemblies of God, a Trinitarian Pentecostal fellowship.)

By definition, if the three persons of the trinity are separate persons, this is tri-theism or the belief in three gods. Tri-theism is rejected among orthodox trinitarians in practice, but not necessarily in spirit.

Most trinitarians deny tri-theism[6], but when asked to explain the trinity doctrine in such a way that it doesn't sound like tri-theism, many beg off with the standard line, "The Godhead is a mystery." How convenient.

The Apostle Paul agreed that the Godhead was a mystery, but to him it was a mystery that was revealed to the Church: *"And without controversy great is the mystery of godliness: God was manifest in the flesh, justified in the Spirit, seen of angels, preached unto the Gentiles, believed on in the world, received up into glory (I Timothy 3:16)."* Paul acknowledged that the Incarnation was incomprehensible in the sense that trying to figure out how God became flesh is impossible, but he affirmed in the clearest possible language that God did become flesh—not the second person in the Godhead, but God Himself.

The definition of the Trinity is fraught with inconsistencies, contradictions, and unexplainable double talk. Consider the following statements from noted trinitarians (bold type added for emphasis):

- Billy Graham: Let's get one thing straight from the beginning and that is that **there is no perfect explanation for the Trinity** of the Godhead. That is a **theological problem** concerning which the most accomplished theologians feel their limitation more than any other doctrine.[7]

- Benjamin Warfield: **The doctrine of the Trinity has never been discovered, and is indiscoverable, by natural reason.** As the doctrine of the Trinity is indiscoverable by reason, so **it is incapable of proof from reason**. The doctrine of the Trinity is given to us in Scripture, not in formulated definition, but in fragmentary allusions. The doctrine of the Trinity is not so much heard as overheard in the statements of Scripture. The Trinity is alluded to rather than asserted. There is again no formal teaching of the doctrine of the Trinity.[8]

- Carl Brumback: How can the revelation of a plurality be reconciled with the revelation of one God? **How can apparent tritheism be harmonized with monotheism? It is beyond the power of reason to comprehend it.** If the New Testament did not exist we could not derive the doctrine of the Trinity from the Old Testament.[9]

- Dr. Herbert Lockyer: **The sacred mystery of the Trinity is one which the light within man could never have discovered**. The Three in One God is **beyond our understanding, beyond our reason**. Three persons yet but one Godhead **cannot be perfectly defined. The Bible does not supply us with any definition of the Trinity. The doctrine of the Trinity is a divine riddle**.[10]

- W. H. T. Dau: The matter expressed by the term Trinity is thus seen to be beyond anything that our mind can conceive, reason out, and explain logically concerning the God of Scripture. **The doctrine of the Trinity is altogether a mystery.**[11]

- Harold O. J. Brown, historian: **It is a simple and undeniable historical fact that the doctrine of the Trinity was not present in a full and well defined, generally accepted from until the fourth or fifth centuries.** The written evidence points to a gradual development of Trinitarianism from the descending triad of Tertullian to the three co-equal, co-eternal persons of the Athanasian Creed.[12]

- E. J. Fortman: **There is no formal doctrine of the Trinity in the New Testament writers, if this means an explicit teaching that in one God there are three co-equal divine persons.**[13]

- See note at end of chapter[14]

The consensus among learned and highly re-nowned trinitarians is that the trinity doctrine is in-discoverable, illogical, unreasonable, contradictory, and inexplicable. Of course it is inexplicable! It is il-logical, unreasonable, and contradictory. Trinitarian theologians admit that the doctrine of the trinity cannot be found in the Bible in clearly stated terms, but rather it can only be "formulated in fragmentary allusions." Let's be honest here. Fragmentary allu-sion is synonymous with man's imagination. The trinity doctrine is man's idea, not God's idea. The trinity doctrine is a man-made doctrine that evolved over time—hundreds of years of time no less. "Divine riddle," preposterous and insulting. It is more like a divine comedy than a "divine riddle." If it wasn't so serious, it would be laughable.

Trinitarian terminology is non-biblical. God is never referred to as a person other than in the con-text of the Incarnation of the invisible God. God is never referred to as being a three in one God. The term "Three Persons in one God" is conspicuously absent from the Bible. The terms God the Son and Eternal Son are non-biblical and directly contradict the biblical terminology that identifies the Man Christ Jesus as the Son of God and the Begotten Son. By definition, begotten and son expressly de-note a beginning. The terms co-equal, co-eternal, and consubstantial are absent from the Bible. Identifying the so called persons of the Godhead as "First Per-son, Second Person, and Third Person" is not only non-biblical, but it implies tri-theism. The words trinity, triune God, and Holy Trinity are not in the Bible.

Some argue that the word "Bible" is not in the Bible, yet Christians believe in the Bible.[15] That is true, but we do not have any doctrines in Christendom based on the word "Bible." A better Scriptural title for the Bible would be the Word of God, but when Christians use the term "Bible," they do so with the understanding that the Bible is the Word of God. The word "Bible" does not conjure up doctrinal thought. It simply designates the 66 canonized books of the Word of God under a single title meaning "The Books." No mystery here. No confusion or historical debates raged over the use of the term "Bible."

Conversely, the word "trinity" is a doctrinal term that profoundly changed the landscape of Christian belief centuries after the end of the New Testament era! The introduction and the official acceptance of the trinity doctrine by the Roman Catholic Church came after much debate in the political, pagan, and theological arenas. To compare the use of the non-biblical terms "Bible" and "Trinity" and imply that since we believe one we can safely believe the other is disingenuous and a cruel distortion of the different contexts in which the two terms are commonly used.

[1] Robert M. Bowmen, Jr. et. al., *What is the Trinity and What Do Christians Believe?*, (Rose Publishing, 1999) pp. 1-7.

[2] Willmington, p. 595.

[3] Finnis Dake, *Dake's Annotated Reference Bible* (Lawrenceville, GA, Dake's Bible Sales, 1963) p. 280.

[4] Bowmen, p. 4.

[5] William R. Ward, *"Processing the Data...It Adds Up to God"* (Pentecostal Evangel, 1966) vol. 2730, p. 12-13.

[6] Willmington, p.595.

[7] Billy Graham, a syndicated column in the *Seattle Post Intelligencer,* 1966.

[8] Benjamin B. Warfield, *International Bible Encyclopedia* entry under *Trinity* (Eerdmans Publishing Co., 1959) p. 3012.

[9] Brumback, p. 95.

[10] Dr. Herbert Lockyer, *All the Doctrines of the Bible* (Zondervan Publishing House, 1969) p. 121-127.

[11] W. H. T. Dau, *the Master Bible* (J. Wesley & Co. Inc., 1967) p. 1369-70.

[12] Harold Brown, *Heresies* (Doubleday & Co.1984) p. 20.

[13] E. J. Fortman, *The Triune God* (Westminster, 1972) p. 32.

[14] Footnotes 5, 7, 8, 10, 11, 12, & 13 were cited from two secondary sources, Symposium on Oneness Pentecostalism 1986 and from lectures at Gateway College of Evangelism 1974.

[15] Bowman et. al., p. 4.

9 trinitarianism or tritheism in disguise

There are essentially two belief systems among trinitarians. The first group believes that the Godhead is a mystery. They cannot explain how God can be three in one in a meaningful way, but instead urge Christians to accept the trinity doctrine by faith. As chronicled in the last chapter, noted trinitarian theologians and scholars acknowledge that the trinity doctrine is not expressly presented in Scripture and it defies reason and logic. Trinitarians admit that the definition of the trinity appears to be contradictory. Nevertheless, trinitarians continue to contend vociferously for the trinity doctrine. When confronted with the inconsistencies of their doctrinal position, most trinitarians throw up their hands in exasperation and fall back on the line, "It is a mystery that must be accepted by faith."

The second group believes the notion that there are three persons in the Godhead. Their visualization of God includes three separate persons: God the Father, God the Son, and God the Holy Ghost. This group believes that, when they pray, they must pray to each member of the Godhead individually while being careful not to slight the other two. They expect to see the three persons of the Godhead if they get to heaven. God the Father will be sitting on the throne, God the Son will be standing or sitting on God the Father's right hand, and God the Holy Ghost will be fluttering around like a dove. In reality this is tritheism, a belief in three gods, as opposed to true trinitarianism, a belief in three persons in one god. This is clearly idolatry and a violation of the first two of the Ten Commandments (Exodus 20:1-5). It is a contradiction of the hundreds of verses of Scripture that express God's absolute oneness. Tritheism is rejected by true trinitarians who contend that only a minority of believers hold to this view.

This being said, in practice, most trinitarians appear to lean more towards tritheism than towards a belief in One God. This is evidenced by the questions they ask regarding the Godhead. When a Oneness believer takes the Biblical position that Jesus is the express image of the invisible God, that Jesus is the Incarnation of the Father and the Holy Spirit, a devout trinitarian will fire off a number of questions similar to the following: Who did Jesus pray to in the garden and on the cross? What about the baptism of Jesus when there was a voice from a heaven, and the Spirit descended like a dove? How do you explain what Stephen saw in Acts 7 when it says he saw Jesus standing on the right hand of God? What about the apostolic greetings in the epistles that reveal a triune God? Who is the "us" referring to in Genesis 1:26?

The very nature of these questions exposes the true nature of trinitarianism: namely, a belief in multiple gods, commonly disguised as persons. There is no need to ask any of the above questions if you actually believe in one God. But if you have the perception that there are three persons in the Godhead, the passages alluded to in the above questions become problematic when presented with the truth of one God.

Who is better able to answer the above questions? The Christian who actually believes in One God or the trinitarian who professes a belief in "one" God, but worships God the Father, God the Son, and God the Holy Ghost? You be the judge.

The Prayers of Jesus

Think about the first question. When Jesus prayed, who was He praying to? First of all the person who asks such a question has in mind that there are two Persons, dare I say gods, present, or there is no need to ask this question. The trinitarian position has the Second Person of the Godhead, God the Son, praying to the First Person of the Godhead, God the Father. There are clearly two Persons or two gods being represented by this position. Second, if this is a case study for trinitarianism, why would one Person of the trinity have to pray to another Person of the trinity? This is a glaring contradiction of a definition that states in part that the three Persons of the Godhead are coequal. If the Second Person of the triune Godhead has to pray to the First Person of the triune Godhead, they are not coequal. Third, can the Second Person of the Godhead even be God if he has to pray to the First Person? By definition God answers prayer, He doesn't have to pray! (This is in fact the position of the Jehovah Witnesses. They believe that Jesus is subordinate to God the Father!)

If a Christian has an understanding of the dual nature of Christ as man and God, he doesn't see multiple persons or gods in the prayer passages, but rather understands that the man Christ Jesus acted out of his human nature when He prayed. But as God, He acted out of His divine nature and answered prayer.

When Jesus prayed in the Garden of Gethsemane, it was with divine foreknowledge. Unlike His disciples, Jesus knew exactly what was coming in the next hours and days. The man Christ Jesus did not want to be flogged, smote, have his beard plucked, and have a crown of thorns smashed upon His head. He did not want to be crucified or run through with a spear. Jesus did not want to be betrayed, mocked, ridiculed and humiliated before His mother, disciples, enemies, and gawking strangers. Yet, at the conclusion of the prayer, Christ subjects the desires of His human nature to His divine nature. The Son of God submitted the will of His flesh to do the will of His Father. But it must be remembered, Jesus was the Father manifested in flesh (Isaiah 9:6, John 10:30, John 14:9, I Timothy 3:16). The prayers of Jesus do not indicate a distinction of persons in the Godhead, but rather a distinction between the human and divine nature of Christ. The man Christ Jesus prayed to the Spirit of the eternal God. But the Spirit of the eternal God dwelt in the man Christ Jesus (Colossians 2:9). He prayed and in a special way He was able to answer His own prayers.

If the prayer life of Jesus teaches a distinction between God the Father and God the Son as the trinitarians suggest, then it must also be concluded that when Jesus died on the cross, the Second Person of the Godhead died! Can part of God die? Did one third of the trinity die on Calvary? Or, if God is the three in one God as trinitarians so whole heartedly contend for, did the whole Trinity die on Calvary? Either way the trinitarian has an unexplainable conundrum. If he admits the Second Person of the Godhead died, he has a multiple god situation. If he admits the triune God died, then God was dead for three days. Unbelievable. Untenable. Unacceptable.

If, on the other hand, you believe in one God with no distinction of persons, the death of Jesus on the cross presents no problem in terms of the Godhead. The flesh of God died on the cross but the Eternal Spirit of God that was in Christ lives forevermore.

The Baptism of Jesus

"And Jesus, when he was baptized, went up straightway out of the water: and, lo, the heavens were opened unto him, and he saw the Spirit of God descending like a dove, and lighting upon him: And lo a voice from heaven, saying, This is my beloved Son, in whom I am well pleased" (Matthew 3:16-17). There it is, the trinity in all of its glory: God the Father, God the Son, and God the Holy Ghost. There are some serious problems, however, with this interpretation. Once again, if the Three Persons of the triune Godhead are present here (Persons that are each called God in their own right), then you have blatant tritheism. God the Father is speaking, God the Son is getting baptized, and God the Holy Ghost is descending like a dove. This sure sounds like 1 + 1 + 1 = 3, not

the 1 x 1 x 1 = 1 position that most trinitarians contend for.

In reality the baptism of Jesus underscores key attributes of God's nature. God is a Spirit (John 4:24) and God is omnipresent (Psalm 139:7-13). While it is true that all the fullness of the Godhead dwells in Jesus (Colossians 2:9), at the Incarnation, God did not cease to be a Spirit, nor did He cease to be omnipresent. God was in Christ (II Corinthians 5:19). God is a Spirit. God is our Father. The Spirit of the Father was in Christ. That is why God could and did say, *"This is my beloved Son, **in whom** I am well pleased."* Notice that God does not say, "with whom," as would be expected if Jesus was the Second Person of the Godhead.

The baptism of Jesus is the inaugural event of Christ's earthly ministry. It must be clearly understood that up until this time, although there may have been some premonitions that Jesus was in some way special, by and large He was raised in obscurity. Had Jesus simply announced that He was God manifest in the flesh, had He simply told people that He was the Messiah, how many people would have believed Him? Today if someone proclaims that they are God, they are turned over to the nearest psychiatric unit. The baptism of Jesus was accompanied by supernatural signs to let John the Baptist and the people of Israel know that Jesus was the Messiah and that He was God with us. The voice of God and the manifestation of the Spirit helped to confirm Christ's true identity. The voice and manifestation of the Spirit do not represent two other Persons in the Godhead. The voice and manifestation of the Spirit represent the omnipresence of God. While on earth, God was still in Heaven (John 3:13). While on earth, Jesus did not abdicate His role as God.

When God speaks to different people in different ways at the exact same time, even though their locations may be scattered across the globe, nobody would suggest that this represents multiple persons in the Godhead. It is understood that God is omnipresent and that He is not limited by time, space, or in this case, a human body. In the baptism of Jesus, the omnipresent God was ministering to different people in different ways to reveal the Messiah, the God of the Old Testament now robed in flesh.

The Right Hand of God

*"So then after the Lord had spoken unto them, he was received up into heaven, and **sat on the right hand of God**" (Mark 16:19).*

*"But he, being full of the Holy Ghost, looked up stedfastly into heaven, and saw the glory of God, and **Jesus standing on the right hand of God**, And said, Behold, I see the heavens opened, and the Son of man standing on the right hand of God. Then they cried out with a loud voice, and stopped their ears, and ran upon him with one accord, And cast him out of the city, and stoned him: and the witnesses laid down their clothes at a young man's feet, whose name was Saul. And they stoned Stephen, calling upon God, and saying, Lord Jesus, receive my spirit. And he kneeled down, and cried with a loud voice, Lord, lay not this sin to their charge. And when he had said this, he fell asleep" (Acts 7:55-60).*

According to Mark 16:19 and a number of other verses of Scripture, Jesus is "sitting" on the right hand of God. According to Stephen (Acts 7:55-60), Jesus is "standing" on the right hand of God. The Trinitarian sees the first two Persons in the triune family represented in these passages, God the Father and God the Son. Three questions immediately come to mind. Does God have a right hand? Is Jesus sitting or standing on God's right hand? Where is God the Holy Ghost while God the Son is sitting and/or standing on God the Father's right hand?

By definition, God is a Spirit (John 4:24) and a Spirit does not have flesh and bones (Luke 24:49) or flesh and blood (Matthew 16:17). By definition, a Spirit is invisible. No one has ever seen God's Spirit (John 1:18). God has manifested Himself at various times and in various forms for the benefit of man, but no man has ever seen the invisible Spirit of God. Therefore, one can conclude that God does not have a right hand.

Under the inspiration of the Holy Ghost, the Bible writers often expressed the infinite and unfathomable God in human terms to help men come to a better understanding of God. For instance, when the plagues were being poured out on Egypt, Pharaoh's magicians warned that this was the *"finger of God" (Exodus 8:19)*. The waters of the Red Sea were gathered *"with the breath of his nostrils" (Exodus 15:8)*. We are admonished in the Book of Proverbs 15:3 that, *"the eyes of the Lord are in every place."* David tells us that *"his ears are open to the cry of the righteous" (Psalm 34:15)*.

Does this mean that Pharaoh's magicians saw God's finger, that Moses and the children of Israel witnessed God blowing his nose to roll back the waters of the Red Sea, or that God has eyes and ears like a man? Absolutely not. To even suggest such a thing is foolishness. These expressions are figurative in nature and are understood as such. The invisible God doesn't have body parts. He doesn't have fingers, a nose, or ears. God is not a giant eyeball. And God doesn't have a right hand!

Exodus 15:6 and 12 were written as expressions of victory and joy over the Israelite deliverance from Egyptian bondage: *"Thy **right hand**, O LORD, is become glorious in power: thy **right hand**, O LORD, hath dashed in pieces the enemy. Thou stretchedst out thy **right hand**, the earth swallowed them."* Does anybody honestly want to argue that the celebrants on that day were rejoicing over seeing God's literal right hand giving them victory? Everyone knows that the usage of "right hand" in the above verses is figurative. God brought victory to Israel by exercising His power and might, not by exposing a literal right hand. If one wants to contend that God has a literal right hand based upon Exodus 15:6 and 15:12, then from the same verses one must also contend that the earth has a mouth and a swallow reflex. Absurd.

The "right hand" of God is referenced over 30 times in the Book of Psalms alone and multiple other times throughout the pages of Scripture. In the Book of Psalms David proclaims, *"Thou wilt shew me the path of life: in thy presence is fulness of joy; at thy **right hand** there are pleasures for evermore"* (Psalm 16:11). "Shew thy marvellous lovingkindness, *O thou that savest by thy **right hand** them which put their* *trust in thee from those that rise up against them"* (Psalm 17:7). These two examples figuratively refer to God's "right hand" in the sense that God bestows the gift of pleasure on those who follow Him and God saves those that put their trust in Him. The other biblical references to God's "right hand" figuratively speak, as do the aforementioned verses, of God's power, authority, and of His desire to save and bless His people.

The trinitarian position argues for a literal right hand. To be consistent then, does the trinitarian equally argue that water has hands? After all Psalm 98:8 reads in part, *"the floods clap their hands?"* How does the trinitarian interpret Isaiah 55:12: *"For ye shall go out with joy, and be led forth with peace:* **the mountains and the hills shall break forth before you into singing**, *and* **all the trees of the field shall clap their hands**"*? Do mountains sing? Do trees clap their hands? Do trees even have their hands? The simple answer to all three questions is "No!" The Prophet Isaiah is using a literary device called an *anthropomorphism* to better illustrate his point. He does not expect his readers to take him literally when it is obvious he is speaking figuratively. If it is understood that the floods and trees don't have hands to clap, it doesn't take a great leap of faith to understand that the invisible God doesn't have a right hand.

The following verses are to be taken literally. There is nothing allegorical or figurative about them. Isaiah 43:11 reads in part, ***"Beside me there is no savior."*** Isaiah 45:5 reads in part, ***"There is no God beside me."*** Isaiah 45:21 reads in part, ***"There is no God else beside me...there is none beside me***."

Isaiah 45:8b emphatically sums up the thoughts of God on this subject, *"Is there a God beside me? Yea, there is no God; I know not any."* What do these verses mean? There is no God beside Him! There isn't a second person of the Godhead standing and/or sitting on His right hand because He doesn't have a right hand. No one sits or stands beside Him because He is God alone.

Jesus is described as the Lamb of God (John 1:29) and the Lion of the Tribe of Judah (Revelation 5:5). Does the trinitarian expect to see a literal Lamb and a literal Lion if they get to heaven? If not, why not? If so, does this add to the number of persons in the Godhead? Does this make Jesus a triune god in his own right (Lamb, Lion, and Son)? Are there animals in the Godhead? Ludicrous and nonsensical!

God made it abundantly clear from the beginning that He was a jealous God (Exodus 20:5, 34:14, Deuteronomy 4:24, 5:9, 6:15, Joshua 24:19) and that He would not share His glory with another (Isaiah 42:8, 48:11). The One God of Israel will not share His glory with supposed second or third persons in the Godhead or anyone else. If you believe that there is another person in the Godhead, then you are boasting that you know more than God knows because He proclaims in Isaiah 44:8: *"Is there a God beside me? Yea, there is no God; I know not any."*

If God did not have a literal right hand in the Old Testament, did He grow one in the New Testament? The Bible states that God never changes (Malachi 3:6 and Hebrews 13:8). God didn't have a literal right hand in the Old Testament and He did not grow one in the New Testament, because God never changes! This is the basis for Christian faith. God is consistent and unchanging.

So what did Steven see in Acts 7:55? Stephen saw Jesus standing in the place of all authority, power, and glory. Stephen only saw Jesus because Jesus is the express image of the invisible God (Hebrews 1:3). When Stephen prayed **he called upon God and said**, "**Lord Jesus** receive my spirit." Stephen only acknowledged one God, and when He called out to this one God, he called Him by name. Stephen cried out to Jesus. Stephen did not pray to a triune God. He did not call out to God the Father and God the Son. Stephen addressed his Lord and God as Jesus. This is the same revelation that Thomas had in John 20:28 when Thomas proclaimed Jesus to be his Lord and God.

In conclusion, is Jesus standing or sitting on the right hand of God? When Jesus is referenced as figuratively sitting on the right hand of God, it represents the finished work of Calvary. Once Jesus had offered Himself on Calvary, the price of redemption had been paid in full. His work as the Man Christ Jesus was done. He could "sit down." As previously mentioned, when Jesus is referenced as standing on the right hand of God, it represents His absolute deity, power, authority, and glory.

The Greetings in the Epistles

Trinitarians often cite the greetings in the epistles to "prove" the trinity doctrine. They recognize a distinction of persons in the Godhead when reading verses such as Romans 1:7, I Corinthians 1:3, and Colossians 1:2. These verses are typical Pauline greetings and are similar in structure and content. Colossians 1:2 is illustrative of Paul's oft-used twofold greeting: *"To the saints **and** faithful brethren in Christ which are at Colosse: Grace be unto you, and peace, from God our Father **and** the Lord Jesus Christ."*

Examination of the Pauline greetings brings more questions than they answer regarding the trinity doctrine. If these verses were intended to impart the trinity doctrine, they fall short. Only two-thirds of the triune Godhead is recognized in these verses, namely God the Father and God the Son. What happened to God the Holy Ghost? If God the Holy Ghost is the third Person of the triune Godhead, then why is He ignored in Colossians 1:2 as well as in most of Paul's other greetings?

H. A. Ironside, a noted 20th Century preacher, theologian, and author of 51 books, wrote a commentary on the Book of Colossians. His remarks about Colossians 1:2a are most enlightening. Ironside observes that the "and" in Colossians 1:2a **does not** suggest that there is a distinction between the "saints" and the "faithful brethren in Christ."[1] There is no implication in Colossians 1:2a that there are two classes of believers. Paul designates Christians as saints by calling and faithful brethren by participatory belief. If the word "and" does not indicate a distinction of persons in Colossians 1:2a, then it doesn't indicate a distinction of persons in 1:2b. God our Father is none other than Jesus Christ!

"And" comes from the Greek word *kai* and can be translated "and" or "even." By replacing the "and" with "even" in Colossians 1:2, the verse would read, *"To the saints **even** the faithful brethren in Christ which are at Colosse: Grace be unto you, and peace,* *from God our Father **even** the Lord Jesus Christ."* Lest one thinks this author is taking unwarranted liberty by replacing "and" with "even," it is not without biblical precedent. *Kai* is translated "and" in II Corinthians 1:2, but "even" in II Corinthians 1:3. *Kai* is also translated "even" in I Corinthians 15:24 (God, even the Father) and I Thessalonians 3:13 (God, even our Father). In the twofold greetings the word "even" adds clarity and gives a more accurate rendering of the verses. The word "and" has elicited a somewhat misleadingly interpretation of these verses and is reflective of the doctrinal beliefs of the trinitarian translators of the King James Version of the Bible.

If the word "and" indicates a distinction of persons in the Godhead, then how does the trinitarian explain Colossians 2:2 which says, *"That their hearts might be comforted, being knit together in love, and unto all riches of the full assurance of understanding, to the acknowledgement of the mystery of God, **and** of the Father, **and** of Christ."* If the trinitarian is consistent in interpretation, and if Colossians 1:2b does in fact make a distinction in persons in the Godhead by employing the word "and," then Colossians 2:2 adds a fourth person. As it reads, Colossians 2:2 gives us God, and the Father, and Christ. Since by definition the Holy Ghost is also part of the triune Godhead, we now have $1 + 1 + 1 + 1 = 4$! The triune god has just become a quartet. Colossians 1:2a proves too little a two person Godhead and Colossians 2:2 proves too much a four person Godhead.

The two-fold greetings acknowledge two of the roles that God plays. "God our Father" represents His role as Father and Creator. The "Lord Jesus Christ" represents His role as the Father manifested in flesh

(I Timothy 3:16). The Jews of Jesus' day did not reject the Father. They rejected the "Son" as the manifestation of the Father. Paul, a Jew, was emphasizing to the Christian community that Jesus Christ was God the Father manifested in flesh and that they must accept Him as such in order to be saved. The Apostle John reiterates this position: **"Whosoever transgresseth, and abideth not in the doctrine of Christ, hath not God. He that abideth in the doctrine of Christ, he hath both the Father and the Son"** (II John 9). How could John make this assertion? Because the Apostle John understood that Jesus was the Incarnation of the Father.

Terms such as God and Father are interchangeable since they are both speaking about one and the same supreme Deity. They may reflect different roles or manifestations, but they don't reflect a distinction in persons. The absence of the Holy Spirit in the two-fold greetings of Paul is consistent with the teaching that God is a Spirit. God is Holy. God is our Father. The Father is the Holy Spirit. In the early stages of the development of the trinity doctrine (see Chapter Ten), the division of persons in the Godhead centered around the division of Father and Son, not the Holy Ghost. The Father and Holy Ghost were considered, even by the early proponents of multiple persons, to be one and the same "person."

Genesis 1:26

"And God said, Let us make man in our image, after our likeness: and let them have dominion over the fish of the sea, and over the fowl of the air, and over the cattle, and over all the earth, and *over every creeping thing that creepeth upon the earth." (Genesis 1:26)*

Here it is again, the triune Godhead. Not exactly. Wherever one verse of Scripture appears to be contradicting another verse of Scripture, there must be a reconciliation of the verses in question. Scripture must interpret Scripture. Before any presumptuous conclusions can be made about the nature of the Godhead based upon Genesis 1:26, one must first reconcile the many other verses of Scripture that clearly teach that One God created man. By reading Genesis 1:27 to Genesis 2:7 we learn that man was created by a "he," not a "them." Genesis 1:27 states, **"So God created man in his own image,** *in the image of God created* **he** *him; male and female created* **he** *them."* Verses 29-30 use the expression **"I have given,"** referencing a single Creator as the gift giver to man. With the exception of the "us" and "our" in Genesis 1:26, all references to the Creator in Genesis 1 and 2 are singular. Genesis 2:7 explicitly identifies one God as the Creator of man: *"And* **the LORD God formed man** *of the dust of the ground, and breathed into his nostrils the breath of life; and man became a living soul."*

Isaiah and Malachi likewise acknowledge only one Creator: *"Thus saith the LORD, thy redeemer, and* **he** *that formed thee from the womb,* **I am the LORD that maketh all things;** *that stretcheth forth the heavens* **alone;** *that spreadeth abroad the earth* **by myself;"** *(Isaiah 44:24).* *"Have we not all* **one father?** *hath* **not one God created** *us?" (Malachi 2:10a).* No triune God is alluded to in these verses.

The Son of God could not have been present at the Creation since the Son was begotten in a manger in Bethlehem several thousand years after the Creation account. God created man in His own image and likeness, the image and likeness of the Son, but He was able to do so because God is able to call those things that are to be as though they already were in existence (Romans 4:17). Man was created in the image and likeness of the Lamb that was slain before the foundation of the world (Revelation 13:8). Even though we know that the Lamb was literally slain at Calvary, the crucifixion had already taken place in the mind of God before the foundation of the world (John 1:1, 1:14). Thus Adam was created in the image and likeness of the begotten Son of God.

There are many possible explanations for the use of the plural "us" in Genesis 1:26, but they do not include multiple persons in the Godhead.

The Jews believed that the "us" referred to the angels who were present at Creation (Job 38:4-7). Although the angels did not take part in the creative act, they were included by God as eyewitnesses of His power.

Some believe that the "us" is a majestic plural in reference to God's royalty. This was a common biblical practice later exercised by other notables. Daniel used the pronoun "we" when he alone interpreted Nebuchadnezzar's dream (Daniel 2:36). King Artaxerxes refers to himself as "I" and "we" in the same passage (Ezra 7:13, 24).

It could be that the LORD God was musing with Himself in Genesis 1:26. Ephesians 1:11 asserts that God counsels after His own will. This is not unlike the man today who says, "Let's see, what am I going to do today?" In Luke 12:19 the rich man talks to himself in the second person: *"And I will say to my soul, Soul, thou hast much goods laid up for many years; take thine ease, eat, drink, and be merry."* This passage in no way suggests that this man was made up of multiple persons.

Whatever one may think about Genesis 1:26, if the "us" was written to indicate the triune nature of God, then why wasn't God clearer? If the intent of this verse was to establish the concept of multiple persons of the Godhead, then the "us" could equally refer to two persons, three persons, four persons, or even a hundred persons in the Godhead. The fact that it is not more explicit suggests that one of the alternative explanations is more accurate, especially in light of the numerous Scriptural references cited that stipulate a single Creator.

Summary

Although trinitarians argue from a doctrinal position that claims there is only one God, their one God is made up of three distinct Persons. This in itself is contradictory. In defense of their indefensible position, the trinitarian maintains that multiple persons of the Godhead were present at Creation, when Jesus was baptized, when Jesus prayed, and when Stephen prayed. They will also cite numerous New Testament verses to underscore their belief in 3 distinct persons in the Godhead including, but not limited to, the apostolic greetings in the epistles, Matthew 28:19 and II Corinthians 13:14. This position smacks of idolatry. This is consistent with the trinitarian belief that the Persons of the triune Godhead are one in unity, but it certainly is not consistent with the belief that God is one in number.

This fact is not lost on orthodox Jews or Moslems. One of the primary reasons the present- day Jews and Moslems, who are staunchly monotheistic, reject Christianity is that they consider the trinity doctrine to be polytheistic (a belief in more that one God). Nobody can think in reasonable terms that 3 = 1 except the trinitarian.

[1] H. A. Ironside, *Philippians, Colossians, Thessalonians* (Loizeaux Brothers, 1975) p. 19-20.

10 the origin of "christian" trinitarianism

The title of this chapter, "The Origin of 'Christian' trinitarianism," is an oxymoron. There is nothing "Christian" about the trinity doctrine. Trinitarianism did not so much as originate in Christianity as it infected Christianity.

When God called Abraham to be the father of a great nation, He was looking for a people who would become the depository for Truth. Through Abraham and his descendants, God spoke to mankind. The nation of Israel became the vehicle whereby God chose to reveal Himself. The pages of the Old Testament testify repeatedly that the God of Israel is absolutely and indivisibly One. The greatest truth and the fundamental creed of ancient Judaism was the Shema: *"Hear, O Israel: The LORD our God is one LORD:" (Deuteronomy 6:4).*

When God ultimately revealed Himself through the Incarnation, it was to and through the Jews. The Apostles were monotheistic Jews. On the Day of Pentecost, the birthday of the Church, the 120 in the Upper Room were monotheistic Jews as were the 3,000 that were added unto the Church that same day. In fact in the early days of the Church, before born again believers were ever called Christians, they were considered just another sect of Judaism, differing only from mainline Judaism by their belief that Jesus was the Incarnation of the one God of the Old Testament.

The Jewish converts to Christianity did not suddenly become trinitarians when they embraced Christ. They continued to contend for the One God of the Old Testament—the God of Abraham, Isaac, and Jacob. The only difference now was that they knew His Name was Jesus. They understood that Jesus was the visible manifestation of the invisible God of the Old Testament.

The Jews that rejected Jesus did not reject Him on the basis of ignorance. They fully understood that Jesus was claiming to be God, but they rejected Jesus because they didn't think man could be God and they were looking for something else in God. They wanted a God that would establish an earthly kingdom and one that would overthrow the Romans. Much to their disappointment, Jesus came to establish a spiritual kingdom. Jesus came to reveal Himself as the Everlasting Father and the Mighty God. For this they crucified Him! What many of the Jews never understood was that Jesus was not just a man trying to be God; He was God trying to be a man for the purpose of redemption!

The New Testament Church was a One God Church. The disciples knew that there was only One Name that could save (Acts 4:12), and they knew that that Name was Jesus. They contended for one Lord, one faith, and one baptism (Ephesians 4:5). The Apostles were keenly aware that the attacks against the early Church would come in the form of attacks against the Godhead. That is why the Apostle Peter warned, *"But there were false prophets also among the people, **even as there shall be false teachers among you, who privily shall bring in damnable heresies, even denying the Lord that bought them**, and bring upon themselves swift destruction"* *(II Peter 2:1-2)*. Jesus was the Lord who had brought them. What better way to sully the gospel than to deny the absolute deity of Jesus Christ? The Godhead became the first target for the enemies of the gospel of Christ.

Note the Apostle Paul's admonition to the Colossians: *"**As ye have therefore received Christ Jesus the Lord, so walk ye in him***: Rooted and built up in him, and stablished in the faith, as ye have been taught, abounding therein with thanksgiving. **Beware lest any man spoil you through philosophy and vain deceit, after the tradition of men, after the rudiments of the world, and not after Christ. For in him dwelleth all the fulness of the Godhead bodily. And ye are complete in him, which is the head of all principality and power:"* *(Colossians 2:6-10)*.

Paul warned that philosophers, pagans, academicians, and pseudo theologians would infiltrate the Church and infect it with false doctrine. The assault on Christianity would come in the form of an unrelenting attack on the full Godhead of Christ. All of Christianity hangs on the premise that Jesus is God manifest in the flesh. To deny that Jesus is the one true God and to deny the absolute deity of Jesus Christ is to undermine the foundation of biblical Christianity.

Jesus forewarned His disciples that they would be **hated for His names sake** (Matthew 10:22, Mark

13:13, Luke 21:17). Jesus was crucified because He claimed to be the King of the Jews, the Messiah, and God manifested in flesh (Matthew 27:11, Luke 23:3, John 18:37). In the Book of Acts chapter 4, Peter and John were commanded not to preach in the Name of Jesus. They could preach whatever they wanted to, but they were forbidden to preach that Name. Why? The aim from the beginning was to defraud Jesus of His true identity, thus stripping the Church of its greatest treasure.

The early disciples were not silenced, hated, or persecuted for casting out devils, healing the sick, working miracles, or speaking in tongues. **They were hated for His Name's sake!** They were hated because they preached that Jesus was the Incarnation of the Old Testament God. The Apostles and early disciples of Christ tenaciously clung to the doctrine of strict monotheism. They recognized that Jesus was the express image of the Old Testament God of Abraham, Isaac, and Jacob.

The "damnable heresy" of II Peter 2:1-2 and Colossians 2:6-10 is to deny the absolute deity of Jesus Christ. Down through the centuries, the enemies of the Church have made every attempt to compromise the integrity of the Godhead by negating the Lordship of Jesus Christ. They have done this by trying to make Him a lesser god or a part of god, all the while denying that He is the only God and the God that sits on the Throne of Revelation 4:2.

The word "spoil" in Colossians 2:8 is in reference to the "spoils of war." How would an invading force plunder or spoil the Church? Paul gives us the answer. False teachers, through philosophy and vain deceit, would steal the truth of Christ's real identity "as so much booty."[1] The Church has no greater treasure than the revelation of the Mighty God in Christ and Paul warned that there would be those who would try to steal this most valuable treasure by perverting or denying the message of the one true God!

The Earliest Trinitarians

Trinitarianism is not a uniquely "Christian" doctrine. Thousands of years before the advent of Christianity, numerous pagan groups throughout the world embraced some form of trinitarianism. In fact it is hard to find any of the ancient religions that do not worship at least some form of a three-fold divine cluster.

The Sumerian culture dates back to approximately 3000 B.C. Although they worshipped multiple gods, the foundation of their religious system was a triad of gods made up of An, the sun god; Enlis, the moon god; and Enki, the earth god. All the other gods they worshiped descended from, or were a combination of, one of these three gods. Some one thousand years later, the religious systems created by the Assyrians and the Egyptians would mirror that of the Sumerians. Although they worshipped a pantheon of gods and goddesses, the central focus of their worship was on a tri-unity of gods. The Assyrian triad consisted of Hadad, the sun god; Atargatis, the moon god; and Nature, the earth god. The Egyptian conglomerate consisted of Amun-Re (or Ra), the sun god; Mut, the earth god; and Khonsu, the moon god. Collectively they were referred to as the Theban Triad. The concept of a tri-unity of gods was "exported" with the marauding armies of the Fertile Crescent to India and China and much later would have an effect on the Japanese. Still later, the triune god belief system of the Assyrians would influence the Greeks and Romans and ultimately the Christians.[2]

The Babylonians advanced the notion of a supreme triad of deities and used the equilateral triangle as a symbol of their trinity. The Hindus, Buddhists, and Taoists all embrace some form of trinitarianism. The Hindu trinity has a corresponding statue of one god with three heads while the Buddhists worship three-headed statues of Buddha.[3]

Since the Bible makes no reference to the trinity doctrine or to a triune god and since the Bible does not employ any of the terms commonly associated with modern day trinitarianism, it must be concluded that "Christian" trinitarianism is more the product of pagan thought and origin than it is of God. Although the "Christian" version of the trinity is slightly more refined and sophisticated than its ancient counterparts, it is little more than a cheap imitation of pagan belief systems.

Trinitarianism, A Formulated Doctrine

The Tyndale House Illustrated Bible Dictionary records that the trinity doctrine was formulated by theologians. This is a fairly representative position held by most Church historians. The opening statement of the dictionary entry under the subheading of "Formulation" states, *"Although **Scripture does not give us a formulated doctrine of the Trinity**, it contains all the elements of which theology has constructed the doctrine."* Under the subheading of

"Derivation" it reads, *"Though **it is not a biblical doctrine in the sense that any formulation of it can be found in the Bible,** it can be seen to underlie the revelation of God, implicit in the OT and explicit in the NT."* According to the dictionary entry, the formulation of the trinity doctrine fell largely on the shoulders of Irenaeus, Origen, Tertullian, Athanasius, and Augustine. These men were the principle theologians recognized as the architects of the trinity doctrine.[4]

The dictionary statements are very troubling on three counts:

1. By their admission, trinitarians accept the position that Scripture does not give us a formulated doctrine of the trinity.
2. Theologians have constructed the doctrine of the trinity based on their private interpretation of the Scriptures.
3. The primary theologians recognized as the architects of the trinity doctrine held wildly divergent views on the Godhead and were not in agreement with each other!

Development of "Christian" Trinitarianism

The Apostles did not believe or teach the doctrine of the trinity, nor did the believers of the First Century Church. They were strict monotheists and recognized that Jesus was their Lord and their God. Timothy, Titus, Aquila and Priscilla, and Apollos, second generation Christian monotheists, likewise made no mention of a triune god and believed in the absolute deity of Jesus Christ. The Post Apostolic Fathers (90-140 A.D.) were equally silent on the subject of the trinity. Mainline Christian believers of the day contended for strict monotheism with no perceptible deviation from Apostolic teaching. Let it be noted that, up until this time, the message of One God had been preached in the Church for over 100 years without serious challenge.

Beginning with the Age of the Greek Apologists (140-180 A.D.), the first rumblings of multiple persons in the Godhead began to appear. Justin Martyr (150 A.D.) was a Greek philosopher turned "Christian" theologian. He was tremendously influenced by the teachings of Socrates and Plato who were in turn greatly influenced by Greek mythology. Plato's concept of god was triune in nature and was comprised of a Supreme God, the Divine Ideas, and the World-Spirit. Plato further elucidated by identifying this pagan trinity as father, begotten son, and unbegotten spirit![5]

Justin Martyr latched on to this philosophical and pagan construct and began to contend for a separation between God the Father and the Word (the Logos of John 1:1), which he identified as the Son. Justin taught that the Son was begotten before creation and was subordinate to the Father. Justin only recognized two persons in the Godhead and one was subordinate to the other. This was one of the first official denials by a theologian of the absolute deity of Jesus Christ. Justin advocated for a triune baptismal formula and is considered to be the first to deviate from the Biblical practice of baptizing in the Name of Jesus. *The New Catholic Encyclopedia* encapsulates this age by saying, *"In the last analysis, the second century theological achievement was lim-*

ited. . . . A trinitarian solution was still in the future."6

The transition from Christian monotheism to trinitarianism had begun. The Old Catholic Age (180-325 A.D.) witnessed the continuing development and advancement of this non-biblical doctrine. Tertullian (210 A.D.) advanced the newly emerging concept by being the first to apply the terms "trinity, three persons, and one substance" to the Godhead. Tertullian subordinated the Son and the Holy Spirit to the Father. Unlike later trinitarians, he did not teach co-equality or co-eternality, nor did he believe that the trinity was permanent, but that it had a beginning and an ending.

Tertullian was less than a stellar example of Christianity and was not highly regarded in his day. He believed that angels were of the same substance as were members of the Godhead, he endorsed celibacy, and he condemned marriage. He cited Matthew 28:19 as the correct baptismal formula and considered triple baptism proper. He was ultimately excommunicated for his extreme beliefs. He also acknowledged that the majority of believers in his day rejected his teaching and embraced the doctrine of One God taught by the Apostles.[7]

Origen (215 A.D.), a contemporary of Tertullian, disagreed with Tertullian on one essential point and advanced the concept of an eternal Son and the eternal generation of the Son. Origen, like Tertullian, continued to relegate Jesus to a subordinate position in the Godhead; thus, Origen did not believe in the co-equality of the members of the Godhead. But unwittingly, by contending for the co-eternality of the

Son, Origen paved the way for the Son to be elevated to a position equal with the Father.[8]

Greatly influenced by Greek philosophy, Origen tended towards mysticism and an allegorical interpretation of the Scripture. He believed in the pre-existence of men's souls, denied the redemptive work of Christ, and believed that evil doers and the devil would be saved. He was eventually excommunicated and cursed officially by the Roman Catholic Church for his heretical beliefs. Consider again that Tertullian and Origen are two of the primary architects of the trinity doctrine, yet both were excommunicated and branded as heretics!

By 325 A.D. there were three sharp divisions among theologians regarding the Godhead. The first group continued to maintain a strict monotheism and fully supported the absolute deity of Jesus Christ. This group was increasingly in the minority. They were silenced and marginalized by the greater debate taking place among the other two divisions. One division, under the leadership of Arius, contended that Jesus was an intermediate created being and thus a lesser god than the Father. He believed in one God but denied that Jesus was that one God. Athanasius, the leader of the other division, advanced the notion that the Father and Son are co-equal, co-eternal, and consubstantial.

The First Council of Nicea was convened in 325 A.D. to settle the dispute between Arius and Athanasius. Like politicians, the two opposing groups met, debated, and voted. In the end, the followers of Athanasius carried the day and trinitarianism became the official position of the Catholic Church. It is interesting to note here that if the followers of Arius had prevailed, we may not be talking about trinitarianism today, but rather binatarianism—a belief in two persons in the Godhead, one being greater than the other.

The Godhead debate instigated by Justin Martyr and others, and advanced by the likes of Tertullian, Origen, Arius, and Athanasius, largely focused on the identity and substance of the Father and the Son. It wasn't until the Council of Constantinople (381 A.D.) that the Holy Spirit was made the official third member of the trinity, heretofore having been largely ignored in the discussions about the Godhead. Imagine. It took almost 350 years, from the Day of Pentecost (the birthday of the Church) for the doctrine of the trinity to be formulated in such a way that it would be recognizable to Christians today. Still the work was not quite done. Roman Catholic theologian Augustine would fine tune the doctrine over the next 50 years. The Nicene and Athanasian Creeds would be modified over the next several centuries to reflect the evolving interpretation of trinitarianism. The Creeds would not be in their final form until at least 500 A.D.

In Conclusion

It is true that the ancient civilizations spoken of in the earlier part of this chapter did not think in terms of one god in three persons, but rather embraced three supreme deities—all other deities being secondary in nature. This is true polytheism. The trinitarians came up with something brand new. In their attempt to have it both ways—worshipping three gods yet claiming to believe in one God—they introduced the trinity doctrine. In this way they were able to appease the pagans, yet continue to call themselves Christians. This is a patently obvious deception.

Most trinitarians will readily admit that the doctrine of the trinity was not formulated in the Bible. Jesus makes no mention of a triune God, nor does He or anyone else introduce Him as the Second Person of the Godhead. Jesus, in fact, claims that He is the Incarnation of the Father and the Holy Spirit (John 14:9, 17). The Apostles make no mention of a triune god nor do they use any of the terms associated with the definition of the trinity doctrine in their New Testament writings. The vast majority of Trinitarians believe that the doctrine of the trinity is inexplicable, not given to reason, contradictory in nature, and a mystery that requires acceptance by faith alone.

Among the architects of trinitarianism, Justin Martyr was a philosopher, Tertullian and Origen were considered heretics and were excommunicated from the church, Athanasius was extremely sensitive to political considerations, and Augustine (considered one of the two greatest Roman Catholic theologians) was greatly influenced by Platonic ideas. Their views on the Godhead differed wildly from one another and, with the possible exception of Augustine, only remotely reflect the definition of trinitarianism that is commonly accepted today. Unquestionably if Justin, Tertullian, and Origen could some how be resurrected today, they would never be allowed to step into the pulpit of a trinitarian church and teach on the Godhead. Their positions fly in the face of orthodox trinitarianism, but are far more closely aligned with the Godhead doctrine of the Jehovah Witnesses!

The Apostle Jude tried to warn the early Church to maintain doctrinal purity by contending for the faith that was once and for all delivered to the saints by Jesus Christ and the Apostles: *"Beloved, when I gave all diligence to write unto you of **the common salvation**, it was needful for me to write unto you, and exhort you that **ye should earnestly contend for the faith which was once delivered unto the saints**. For there are certain men crept in unawares, who were before of old ordained to this condemnation, ungodly men, turning the grace of our God into lasciviousness, and **denying the only Lord God, and our Lord Jesus Christ**"* (Jude 4-5). If we sincerely want to know what the Bible teaches about the Godhead, Jude admonished the Church to look back to the Word of God for an answer. The Trinitarians conversely urge us to look forward to the formulations of men, man-made creeds, and the Roman Catholic Church for the authoritative word on the Godhead.[9] This is backward and frightening in its implications. It leaves the door wide open for every wind of doctrine. It implies that the Apostles did not have the full revelation of the Godhead and that the New Testament was completed without the centerpiece doctrine of the Church. Is this even plausible or acceptable on any level?

The real irony of the trinitarian position is that, although most trinitarians agree that the doctrine of the trinity evolved over a period of hundreds of years, they still contend that the trinity doctrine is a Bible doctrine! How can that be? Either the trinity doctrine was formulated by men or it came from the Bible.

Since we know that it did not come from the Bible, that it was never articulated by Jesus or the Apostles, it cannot, and must not, be considered a Bible doctrine.

---

[1] W. E. Vine, *Expository Dictionary of Bible Words,* Thomas Nelson Publishing, 1985.

[2] Robert McFarland, *The History and Origin of the Trinity,* (McFarland Publishing, 2005) pp. 29-55.

[3] Bernard, p. 264-265.

[4] J. D. Douglas (editor), *The Illustrated Bible Dictionary – Trinity entry,* (Inter-Varsity Press, Tyndale House Publishers, 1980) vol. 3, pp. 1597-99

[5] David Huston, *The Light of Pentecost* (Antioch Publishers, 1989) pp. 29-32.

[6] Holy *Trinity, New Catholic Encyclopedia*, (McGraw Hill, 1967) pp. 295-305.

[7] Bernard, pp. 268-270.

[8] Ibid., pp. 270-271.

[9] Nathaniel Urshan, et. al., *Symposium on Oneness Pentecostalism,* (Word Aflame Press, 1986) pp. 63-64.

11 why does any of this really matter?

The tone of this book, as announced in the preface, has been provocative. If you have read this far, some might even suggest, confrontational. Yet, how else would you challenge someone to rethink their position on a doctrine that has been entrenched in Christianity for so long that it is rarely given a second thought? It has been my experience over the years that when it comes to doctrine, people do not understand subtlety. A straight forward and direct approach seems to me to be far more impacting.

As in preaching, "good" is relative. Success cannot be measured on a popularity meter. The successful preacher preaches people to a point of decision. Regardless of whether the listener responds positively or negatively to the message, if the listener makes a decision, then the preacher was successful. We would all like people to respond positively to the messages we preach, but worse than a negative response is no response at all. This book was written to underscore and bolster the faith of those who already believe the message of the Mighty God in Christ, but more importantly it was written to bring our trinitarian counterparts to a point of decision regarding the Mighty God in Christ.

To know God is to at least understand the nature of the Godhead. The mystery of the Incarnation, the mystery of God in Christ, the mystery of man and God coming together in flesh is not completely fathomable for any of us, but the nature of the mystery was revealed to us. God was manifest in flesh (I Timothy 3:16), God was in Christ reconciling the world onto Himself (II Corinthians 5:19), and all the fullness of the Godhead dwelt in Jesus bodily (Colossians 2:9). Jesus is the Almighty God (Revelation 1:8, 4:8) and there is no other God beside Him. He is absolutely and indisputably the One God of the Bible. Understanding the Godhead opens the door to salvation. To misunderstand the Godhead will lead to eternal destruction.

Did I go too far with that last remark? Consider the words of Jesus in John 8:20, 23-24: *"Then said they unto him, Where is thy Father? Jesus answered, Ye neither know me, nor my Father:* **if ye had known me, ye should have known my Father also**. *And he said unto them, Ye are from beneath; I am from above: ye are of this world; I am not of this world. I said therefore unto you, that ye shall die in your sins: for* **if ye believe not that I am he, ye shall die in your sins.***"* Jesus did not mince any words with those that were challenging Him. The antecedent for the pronoun "he" in verse 24 is the "Father" from verse 21. Jesus let the Pharisees know that if they didn't believe that He was the Father Incarnate, they would die in their sins. Jesus spoke with authority and finality. If you fail to understand that when you see Jesus you are seeing the Father, according to Jesus, you can't be saved!

Man has a tendency to look for loopholes. God has a way of closing the loopholes. When Noah and his family got on the Ark to escape the flood, the rest of the world perished; by some estimates over 3,000,000 people died! The Bible records that God "shut the door" on the Ark. What God shuts, no man can open. As Noah and his family listened to the terror of death, the clawing of fingernails on the sides of the Ark, the pounding on the door, and the wails of the dying, my guess is that they would have had "compassion" on the lost and dying and opened the door so that more might be saved. But God would not be party to this folly. Man had been given space to repent. Man had been given a chance to willingly get on the ark. Man had been given a chance to believe the Word of God. But when man refused, judgment day came. Judgment day always comes.

Jesus said, **"If ye believe not that I am he, ye shall die in your sins!"**

Sodom and Gomorrah were destroyed with all the inhabitants therein. There must have been some "good" people in Sodom and Gomorrah. What about the church goers, the girl scout and boy scout leaders, the PTA volunteers, the organ donors, the volunteer shelter workers, and the tree huggers? Our righteousness and goodness is as filthy rags before the Lord (Isaiah 64:6).

Jesus said, *"If ye believe not that I am he, ye shall die in your sins!"*

Achan (Joshua 7:19-26), the man who picked up sticks on the Sabbath day (Numbers 15:32-36), those that died while wondering in the Wilderness, King Saul, and King Uzziah are representative of those who God judged for their disobedience. Lest one think that the judgment of God is exclusively reserved for the Old Testament unfaithful, consider the end of Ananias and Sapphria. The Apostle Paul reiterated the words of Jesus in II Thessalonians 1:7-9: *"And to you who are troubled rest with us, when the Lord Jesus shall be revealed from heaven with his mighty angels, In flaming fire **taking vengeance on them that know not God, and that obey not the gospel of our Lord Jesus Christ:** Who shall be punished with everlasting destruction from the presence of the Lord, and from the glory of his power;"*.

Jesus said, *"**If ye believe not that I am he, ye shall die in your sins" (John 8:24)!***

Why was Jesus so adamant about this? Because Jesus knew and understood that an improper understanding of the Godhead would lead to a perversion of the very plan of salvation.

Matthew 28:19

No discussion on the Godhead would be complete without an interpretation of Matthew 28:18-20: *"And Jesus came and spake unto them, saying, All power is given unto me in heaven and in earth. Go ye therefore, and teach all nations, **baptizing them in the name** of the Father, and of the Son, and of the Holy Ghost: Teaching them to observe all things whatsoever I have commanded you: and, lo, I am with you alway, even unto the end of the world. Amen."*

The operative word of Matthew 28:19 is **"name."** In this case it is as important to notice what the verse does not say as well as what it says. The verse does not use the plural word "names" but rather uses the singular word "name." The Apostles were commanded to baptize in the singular name of the Father, Son, and Holy Ghost. That begs the questions, what is the singular name of the Father, Son, and Holy Ghost? What name did the Apostles use in baptism? What is the only New Testament name associated with salvation? What is God's name? The answer to all four questions is, JESUS!

JESUS is the name of the Father (John 5:43), JESUS is the name of the Son (Matthew 1:21), and JESUS is the name of the Holy Ghost (John 14:26). Father, Son, and Holy Ghost all describe JESUS, the one God of the Bible. But Father, Son, and Holy Ghost are not names for God. The Apostles only and always baptized in the name of JESUS (Acts 2:38, 8:16, 10:48, and 19:5). Acts 4:12 reads, *"**Neither is there salvation in any other: for there is none other name under heaven given among men, whereby we must be saved.**"* What name was being referred to in Acts 4:12? The only possible answer to that question is JESUS.

Some suggest that the Apostles were in error when they baptized people in the name of Jesus. That is an untenable position for a Bible believing Christian: *"**All scripture is given by inspiration of God**, and is profitable for doctrine, for reproof, for correction, for instruction in righteousness:" (II Timothy 3:16).* If the Apostles were somehow in error, then it undermines the credibility of the entire New Testament since the Apostles wrote the New Testament! Some would suggest that it is better to obey the words of Jesus in Matthew 28:19 than the words of Peter in Acts 2:38. That is the whole point. When they baptized in Jesus' name, the Apostles were obeying Christ's command to baptize in the name of the Father, Son, and Holy Ghost. The name of the Father, Son, and Holy Ghost is JESUS!

If one believes in a triune god, then a triune baptismal formula seems reasonable. But consider the baptismal formula that employs the words, "Father, Son, and Holy Ghost." First, it is a no name baptism! Can a no name baptism remit sin? Father, Son, and Holy Ghost are titles. I am a father, son, and husband, but I cannot sign legal documents using my titles or roles on the signature line and make them valid. Our signatures require a name. Baptism requires a name. JESUS is the name. Second, there is no biblical precedent for using a baptismal formula that employs the words Father, Son, and Holy Ghost. Christian baptism was always administered in the name of JESUS in the Bible. There is no efficacy in a no name baptism. The participant goes down in the water a dry sinner and comes up a wet sinner! Without the Name, Christian baptism is powerless!

It is astounding to me that Christians pray, cast out devils, heal the sick, and perform miracles all in the name of Jesus. But when they get baptized, they use the titles Father, Son, and Holy Ghost. This is in direct opposition to the command of Colossians 3:17: *"And whatsoever ye do in word or deed, **do all in the name of the Lord Jesus**, giving thanks to God and the Father by him."*

Some attempt to legitimize the triune baptism formula of Father, Son, and Holy Ghost by tacking the words, "in Jesus name" on at the end. That is a dead give away that they just don't get it. If a person recognizes that Jesus is God, being baptized in the name of Jesus is not only biblical, but logical, and it doesn't require the repetition of the triune formula.

Some ministers will admit that Jesus Name baptism is the legitimate baptism of the New Testament Church, but they see no need to be re-baptized, nor will they re-baptize their members. Many of them, such as Martin Luther and other Reformers, recognized that baptism in Jesus' Name was biblical, but in practice continued to use the traditional triune formula of the Roman Catholic Church.

Why does any of this matter? Do we really think we can modify God's plan of salvation and still be saved? Peter said, *"Baptism doth also now save us" (I Peter 3:21)*! Jesus said, *"He that believeth and is baptized shall be saved; but he that believeth not shall be damned" (Mark 16:16)*. You can't get any plainer than that. If baptism saves us, and the Bible is adamant that it does, it behooves us to use the correct baptismal formula.

In Acts 19, the disciples of John the Baptist met up with the Apostle Paul. When he realized that they didn't have the Holy Spirit, he immediately questioned their baptism. Even though they were believers, even though they were disciples, even though they had already been baptized, they had never heard of Jesus Name baptism. Paul then explained the essentiality of Jesus Name baptism to them and Luke records the result of Paul's message: ***"When they heard this, they were baptized in the name of the Lord Jesus"*** *(Acts 19:5)*. If you haven't been baptized in Jesus' Name, do not delay. Find someone that will baptize you using the biblical formula for baptism.

Roman Catholics and Triune Baptism, Are You One of Them?

At the Second Vatican Council (1962-1963) Pope John XXIII stated that the Roman Catholic Church was extending open arms to "all of our daughters," which means to anyone that has not forsaken our baptism. "Our baptism" is a direct reference to a triune baptismal formula. Even the Roman Catholic Church recognized that, in the beginning, baptism was performed in the Name of Jesus and that triune baptism was a definite product of the Roman Catholic Church.

The Reformation, which was in it self a protest against Roman Catholic doctrine and papal authority, succeeded only to the extent that the Protestant Reformers were willing to relinquish Roman Catholic doctrines and traditions. So although the Reformers reckoned that, among other things, "the just shall live by faith," that papal authority was not synonymous with God's authority, that the Bible was the final authority in all matters of doctrine, and that communion was symbolic in nature, they did not disavow the Roman Catholic teaching on the triune Godhead or triune baptism. Taking his cue from the Protestant failure to deny the Roman Catholic positions on the Godhead and baptism, Pope John XXIII "included" mainline Protestants and Evangelicals in the Roman Catholic family, even if he considered them to be "separated brethren."[1] Pope John XXIII, along with other Roman Catholic theologians, felt that the uniting factor in any ecumenical movement would be the commonality shared on the triune Godhead and triune baptism. How sad that those who ignited the Reformation were not willing to reevaluate and abandon all Roman Catholic traditions and creeds, especially those relative to the Godhead and baptism.

What we believe matters. A person can be quite sincere in their belief, but still be sincerely wrong! It is of utmost importance whether we believe in the God of the Bible or the manufactured triune god(s) of creeds, Roman Catholic dogma, and tradition. The Apostles didn't teach the doctrine of the trinity, nor did they use a triune baptismal formula. The Apostle Paul warned, *"But though we, or an angel from heaven, preach any other gospel unto you than that which we have preached unto you, let him be ac-cursed. As we said before, so say I now again, If any man preach any other gospel unto you than that ye have received, let him be accursed"* (Galatians 1:8-9). This two-fold repetition by the Apostle Paul under-scored the importance placed on remaining true to the message that was once and for all delivered to the saints (Jude 4-5).

In the words of the Prophet Elijah: *"How long halt ye between two opinions? if the LORD be God, fol-low him: but if Baal, then follow him. And the people answered him not a word"* (I Kings 18:21). The same can be said today. If Jesus is God, serve Him. If the trinity is god, then serve the trinity. But remember, this is one time the majority doesn't rule. Elijah went up against the 450 prophets of Baal and came out victorious. One day the God that answers by fire will judge all of the false gods of man's imagination.

The Apostle John said of the Jews, *"He came unto his own, and his own received him not"* (John 1:11). The Jews rejected Christ for a number of reasons, not the least of which was that they did not believe He was God. They knew and understood that He claimed to be God, but they rejected those assertions. Their unbelief and denial of the absolute deity of Jesus Christ, however, did not change the identity of Christ. Jesus is still God and beside Him there is no other.

The words of the Prophet Zechariah are most enlightening on this subject: *"In that day shall the **LORD** defend the inhabitants of Jerusalem; and he that is feeble among them at that day shall be as David; and the house of David shall be as **God**, as the angel of the LORD before them. And it shall come to pass in that day, that I will seek to destroy all the nations that come against Jerusalem. And I will pour upon the house of David, and upon the inhabitants of Jerusalem, the spirit of grace and of supplications: and they shall look upon **me** whom they have pierced, and they shall mourn for him, as one mourneth for his only son, and shall be in bitterness for him, as one that is in bitterness for his firstborn" (Zechariah 12:8-10).* The antecedents to the pronouns "I, I, and me" in this passage are LORD (Jehovah) and God (Elohim). Who is the LORD and God of Zechariah 12:8-10? JESUS! The God that the Jews rejected in the New Testament was the Incarnate God of the Old Testament. At the day of their deliverance, the children of Israel will look upon their LORD and God when they see the one whom they pierced. Who did they pierce? JESUS!!! Jesus is the express image of the one God of Israel. Jesus is God alone.

---

[1] David Bernard, *A History of Christian Doctrine, Volume 3* (Word Aflame Press, 1999) pp.230-233.

12 john 3:16

"For God so loved the world, that he gave his only begotten Son, that whosoever believeth in him should not perish, but have everlasting life" (John 3:16).

John 3:16 is the best known and most frequently quoted verse of Scripture in the entire Bible. Unfortunately, it is also one of the most misunderstood. The popular misinterpretation suggests that one divine person of the Godhead (God the Father) begot the second person in the Godhead (God the Son) for the purpose of redemption. Some have also used this verse to "preach another Gospel," the Gospel of easy believism. Invariably, when ones understanding of the Godhead is wrong, his understanding of the New Testament plan of salvation is wrong as well.

While trinitarians erroneously point out that John 3:16 references two members of a triune Godhead, they fail to link John 3:16 with I John 3:16. Does John 3:16 reference two persons in the Godhead? No! How do we know? By reading I John 3:16: *"Hereby perceive we the love of **God**, because he **laid down his life for us**: and we ought to lay down our lives for the brethren."* Who laid down His life for us? God did! Which God? God the Father, God the Son, or God the Holy Ghost? We know that Jesus laid down His life for us. I John 3:16 therefore asserts that Jesus is God. Since there is no God beside God (I Samuel 2:2, Isaiah 44:6, Hosea 13:4) and since Jesus is God, John is not making a distinction between persons in the Godhead in John 3:16, but he is making a distinction between the Spirit of God and the flesh of God.

The Father so loved the world that he gave his own Son (flesh) that whosoever would believe in Him would not perish, but would have everlasting life. The term "Son" always refers to God's manifestation in flesh. God loved fallen mankind so much that He became flesh (John 1:14) so that He could be "God with us" (Isaiah 7:14, Matthew 1:23). God ultimately offered up the only sacrifice that could save us from our sins, His own flesh. The flesh of God did what the Spirit of God could not do. The flesh or Son could die and become our sacrifice, but the Spirit of God in the Son could not die. That is why Jesus could say, *"Destroy this temple* (my body, John 2:21), *and in three days I will raise it up" (John 2:19).* The flesh or Son of God died on the Cross, but the Spirit of God in the Son raised the Son at the Resurrection: *"God was in Christ reconciling the world unto himself" (II Corinthians 5:19),* not to another God or to another person in the Godhead, but unto Himself.

If John 3:16 is speaking of two separate persons in a triune Godhead, it is problematic for the trinitarian on two counts. First, two does not equal one! If God the Father, who by trinitarian definition is not God the Son, sends God the Son, who by trinitarian definition is not God the Father, you now have two distinct God-like beings. That is idolatry. It is not a representation of two in one; it is a clear distinction between one divine person called God the Father and a second divine person called God the Son. A cogent argument cannot be made for a belief in one God based upon the trinitarian interpretation of this verse.

The second problem that arises from a trinitarian interpretation of this verse is that it becomes profoundly hard to believe that God the Father is a loving God. If the First Person of the Godhead sends the Second person of the Godhead to die for our sins, the sacrifice does not appear to be motivated by love, but rather by selfishness. It smacks of cowardice and brutality. In other words, if I offered to take the punishment you had coming for a crime committed, and then worked out an exchange whereby my beloved first born son's life would be sacrificed to pay the penalty for your crime, you might be relieved that someone was paying the price for your crime. However, I seriously doubt you would look at me as a loving father. What loving father willingly gives up the life of his child as a substitute for meeting his own responsibility?

God's View of Child Sacrifice

The one God of Deuteronomy 6:4 abhorred the very thought of child sacrifice. Child sacrifice was tantamount to the worst possible evil that man could inflict upon his own offspring. God "hated" child sacrifice, called it an "abomination," and expressly forbade the children of Israel from participating in such a heinous act. (Deuteronomy 12:31). There is no subtlety in the Word of God when it comes to God's absolute loathing of the practice of child sacrifice.

Jeremiah 7:31 is a powerful and revealing expression of God's utter contempt for child sacrifice: *"And they have built the high places of Tophet, which is in the valley of the son of Hinnom,* **to burn their sons and their daughters in the fire; which I commanded them not, neither came it into my heart.***"* Although the practice of child sacrifice had been forbidden by God in at least 17 other verses of Scripture, this verse reveals the depth of disgust over the practice. God is so shocked by the depravity of those who used children in sacrificial rituals that He laments that the idea of child sacrifice had never even crossed His own mind. He never even imagined that human beings would engage in such wickedness!

Man's propensity for evil seems to know no bounds. Eerily reminiscent of Noah's day, God's prohibition against child sacrifice was necessitated by man's wicked imaginations: *"And GOD saw that the wickedness of man was great in the earth, and that every imagination of the thoughts of his heart was only evil continually. And it repented the LORD that he had made man on the earth, and it grieved him at his heart"* (Genesis 6:4-5). God was grieved by the gruesome spectacle of child sacrifice. II Kings 16:3 calls child sacrifice the "abominations of the heathen." It was certainly not enjoined under any circumstances for the children of Israel. (How could anyone wonder how God views abortion—the modern day slaughter of the innocents?)

Now if it is true that God does not change (Malachi 3:6) and He is the same yesterday, today, and forever (Hebrews 13:8), when did God acquire an appetite for child sacrifice? Think about it. If Person Number One (called the Father) sacrifices Person Number Two (called the Son), it is child sacrifice! Are we to believe that God the Father expresses His love for us by sending a Second Person called God the Son to be brutally beaten and crucified on our behalf? If so, does anybody want to call God a hypocrite for violating His own prohibition against child sacrifice?

The truth of the matter is that the Bible teaches, *"Greater love hath no man than this, that a man lay down his life for his friends" (John 15:13)*. There is no implication here that a man can offer a family member as a sacrifice to express his love. God did not offer some supposed secondary deity to be the sacrifice for our sins; He came Himself. The Bible says so: *"Hereby perceive we the love of **God**, because he **laid down his life for us:** and we ought to lay down our lives for the brethren" (I John 3:16)*! That was the entire purpose of the Incarnation—God with us, so God could save us through His personal sacrifice. God was manifested in flesh (I Timothy 3:16) for the purpose of redemption. God loved us so much that He humbled Himself to become a man so that He Himself could be the sacrifice for our sins. Now that is real love.

Taking John 3:16 in Context

A second fundamentally flawed belief has arisen from the erroneous interpretation of John 3:16. The Apostle John does not endorse or advance a triune god mentality in John 3:16 nor does he advocate for a plan of salvation that simply requires belief. The Apostle James states, *"Thou believest that there is one God; thou doest well: the devils also believe, and tremble" (James 2:19).* Two substantive points can be derived from this verse. One, the devils believe in one God and they tremble at this truth. The devils do not tremble over the formulated doctrine of a triune god. Two, no one would suggest that the devils can be saved just because they believe. Well, almost no one. Origen, one of the people responsible for the development of the trinity doctrine did believe that the devils would be saved.

The popular mantra given as the plan of salvation in most evangelical and fundamentalist churches today is "Accept the Lord as your personal savior and you shall be saved." There may be a "sinner's prayer" attached to the plan, but basically belief and confession are the sole requirements for salvation. John 3:16 and Romans 10:9 are two of the proof texts for this doctrinal position.

The "believe and you shall not perish" portion of John 3:16 has been misconstrued to convey the message that belief alone is sufficient for salvation. As pointed out, the devils believe but are not saved. You can believe and not be saved. Although belief is necessary for salvation, when John 3:16 is taken in context, there are other requirements that are also necessary for salvation. If you are going to properly interpret John 3:16, it is imperative that you read the verses preceding John 3:16:

"There was a man of the Pharisees, named Nicodemus, a ruler of the Jews: The same came to Jesus by night, and said unto him, Rabbi, we know that

*thou art a teacher come from God: for no man can do these miracles that thou doest, except God be with him. Jesus answered and said unto him, Verily, verily, I say unto thee, **Except a man be born again, he cannot see the kingdom of God.** Nicodemus saith unto him, How can a man be born when he is old? can he enter the second time into his mother's womb, and be born? Jesus answered, Verily, verily, I say unto thee, **Except a man be born of water and of the Spirit, he cannot enter into the kingdom of God.** That which is born of the flesh is flesh; and that which is born of the Spirit is spirit. **Marvel not that I said unto thee, Ye must be born again.** The wind bloweth where it listeth, and thou hearest the sound thereof, but canst not tell whence it cometh, and whither it goeth: so is every one that is born of the Spirit" (John 3:1-9).*

There can be little doubt that in His discourse with Nicodemus, Jesus made it abundantly clear that to be saved, a person must be born again. Jesus warned Nicodemus that if he was not born of the water and of the Spirit, he would never see the kingdom of God and would never enter the kingdom of God (John 3:3, 5). The drama of this passage cannot be overstated. Nicodemus is not some unregenerate heathen. He is a highly respected Pharisee and a ruler of the Jews. He is a believer! Yet, Jesus commanded him to be born again.

How is one born again? The new birth is comprised of repentance, baptism in the Name of Jesus Christ, and receiving the gift of the Holy Spirit with the evidence of speaking in other tongues (Acts 2:38). To be sure, belief is an essential prerequisite for the new birth, but the new birth is incomplete with belief alone.

Jesus said, **"He that believeth and is baptized shall be saved**; *but he that believeth not shall be damned" (Mark 16:16).* In the Apostle Peter's first message to the New Testament Church, the listeners cried out, **"What shall we do**?" Peter responded with, **"Repent,** *and* **be baptized every one of you in the name of Jesus Christ** *for the remission of sins, and* **ye shall receive the gift of the Holy Ghost"** *(Acts 2:37-38).* In the same message Peter had already stated, *"And it shall come to pass, that whosoever shall call on the name of the Lord shall be saved" (Acts 2:21).* But if a simple calling of His name was sufficient for salvation, those who heard the message did not have to ask Peter, "What shall we do?" They understood that more was required than simply calling on His name and they wanted to know what more they had to do. Peter explained that His name, the Name of Jesus, had to be called or invoked over them and this could only be done in baptism. Peter was adamant about the importance of baptism. In I Peter 3:21, he declared that baptism saves us: *"The like figure whereunto even* **baptism doth also now save us** *(not the putting away of the filth of the flesh, but the answer of a good conscience toward God,) by the resurrection of Jesus Christ:"*!

In today's Christian climate of easy believism, Cornelius of Acts 10 fame would already be saved. It was said of him that he was devout, feared God, gave much in the offering, and prayed always. In other words, he was a believer and undoubtedly a strong candidate to be a deacon or board member. But when Peter preached to Cornelius, even after Cornelius was filled with the Holy Spirit and began to speak in other tongues, Peter "**commanded**" him to be baptized (Acts 10:48)!

In Acts 19:1-6, when the Apostle Paul met up with some disciples at Ephesus, he discussed their new birth experience. When he realized that they had not received the Holy Spirit, he immediately questioned their baptism. These believers had submitted to the baptism of John the Baptist, but not to Jesus Name baptism. The Apostle Paul then re-baptized these believers in the Name of Jesus.

Baptism is not the tail on the dog. It is not the outward sign of an inner work. Baptism saves us (Mark 16:16, I Peter 3:21) and baptism is for the remission or washing away of our sins (Acts 2:38). To be born of water is to be baptized in Jesus Name. Jesus Name baptism is essential for New Testament salvation.

The new birth is incomplete without water baptism and without the infilling of the Holy Spirit. The Apostle Paul emphatically stated in Romans 8:9, *"But ye are not in the flesh, but in the Spirit, if so be that the Spirit of God dwell in you. Now if any man have not the Spirit of Christ, he is none of his."* Jesus told Nicodemus that there would be a sound accompanying the infilling of the Spirit (John 1:8). In Acts 2:4, the one-hundred twenty who were gathered in the upper room waiting for the promise of God were **all** filled with the Holy Spirit and they **all** spoke in other tongues. Speaking in tongues was the sound or evidence of being filled with the Holy Spirit. Peter, speaking of the promise, stated, *"For the promise is unto you, and to your children, and to all that are afar* *off, even as many as the Lord our God shall call"* (Acts 2:39).

Throughout the pages of the Book of Acts, those that heard the message of Christ were baptized in Jesus Name and filled with the Holy Ghost as evidenced by speaking in other tongues (See Acts 2, 8, 10, and 19). You must be born of the Spirit to be saved. When you are born of the Spirit, you will speak in other tongues. The infilling of the Holy Ghost is essential for New Testament salvation. When you buy a pair of shoes you do not have to ask for the tongues because the tongue come with each shoe. When you get the Holy Ghost, tongues will accompany the experience.

Now back to Romans 10:9: *"That if thou shalt confess with thy mouth the Lord Jesus, and shalt believe in thine heart that God hath raised him from the dead, thou shalt be saved."* Romans 10:9 was written to the "saints" or born again believers in Rome (Romans 1:7), not to the unsaved in Rome. To base the formula for salvation upon Romans 10:9 is to take a verse written to one group of people and apply it to another group with disastrous results. This misapplication leads to a watered-down version of the gospel which is completely divorced from the New Testament plan of salvation as found in the Book of Acts.

Even so, the new birth can be found in the Book of Romans. Romans 6:4-5 stresses the essentiality of Jesus Name baptism to those that had already been baptized in Rome: *"Know ye not, that so many of us as **were baptized into Jesus Christ** were baptized into his death? **Therefore we are buried with him by baptism** into death: that like as*

Christ was raised up from the dead by the glory of the Father, even so we also should walk in newness of life." Romans 8 is a discourse on the importance of being filled with the Holy Spirit. Romans 10:9 then is an exposition of what happens in salvation, but, if you want to know how to be saved, read the Book of Acts. The Book of Acts is the historical record of the birth of the Church and of how others were subsequently added to the Church.

Although the focus of this book is on the Godhead, the subject of the Godhead is forever united with the message of salvation. When one understands that Jesus is God, then it only makes sense to baptize in the Name of Jesus and follow through with the plan of salvation as given to us by Jesus.

The Thief on the Cross

One of the arguments against following through with the new birth as commanded by Jesus and preached by the Apostles is the account of the thief on the cross as recorded in Luke 23:39-43:

"And one of the malefactors which were hanged railed on him, saying, If thou be Christ, save thyself and us. But the other answering rebuked him, saying, Dost not thou fear God, seeing thou art in the same condemnation? And we indeed justly; for we receive the due reward of our deeds: but this man hath done nothing amiss. And he said unto Jesus, Lord, remember me when thou comest into thy kingdom. And Jesus said unto him, Verily I say unto thee, To day shalt thou be with me in paradise."

Because this man was saved without experiencing the new birth, some contend that the new birth is not necessary and that baptism is an outward sign of an inner work—a ritual or rite that is not essential to salvation. The point that is overlooked, however, is that when Jesus saved this man, the Church had not yet been born! The gospel is the death, burial, and resurrection of Jesus Christ. We identify with Christ's death in repentance, burial in water baptism, and resurrection with the infilling of the Holy Spirit. Since Jesus acted on behalf of the repentant thief on the cross before His death, burial, and resurrection, the New Testament plan of salvation had not yet been implemented: *"For where a testament is, there must also of necessity be the death of the testator. For a testament is of force after men are dead: otherwise it is of no strength at all while the testator liveth" (Hebrews 9:16-17).* Until Jesus died, was buried, and rose again, the testament could not be executed. The repentant thief on the cross was not saved under the New Testament dispensation of grace so he cannot be used as an example to justify salvation outside the parameters of the new birth during the Church Age.

(NOTE: For a more complete exegesis on John 3:16, I recommend David A. Huston's Book, *"The Real Message of John 3:16,"* available through Rosh Pinnah Publications, P.O. Box 337, Carlisle, PA 17013-0337.)

13

when you say "jesus," you have said it all!

The Apostle Peter admonished, *"But sanctify the Lord God in your hearts: and be ready always to give an answer to every man that asketh you a reason of the hope that is in you with meekness and fear:" (I Peter 3:15)*. It was the intent of this book to give an answer for the hope that lies within me—that one day we will see our Lord and Savior, Jesus Christ, face to face. To know God is to know His Name. To know God is to know and understand that Jesus is God and beside Him there is no other.

Moses began his ministry at a burning bush when God revealed Himself as the Self Existent One—the I AM THAT I AM: *"And God said moreover unto Moses, Thus shalt thou say unto the children of Israel, The LORD God of your fathers, the God of Abraham, the God of Isaac, and the God of Jacob, hath sent me unto you: **this is my name for ever**, and **this is my memorial unto all generations"** (Exodus 3:15)*. God's declaration to Moses was particularly powerful and underscored His absolute oneness. At the pronouncement of His name in Exodus 3:14, the singular pronouns in the title, I AM THAT I AM, leave little room to maneuver and finagle the Godhead into a multi-person monstrosity. The LORD

God of Israel proclaimed that His name was singular and that this would be a memorial for all generations. The singular Name of our God is JESUS.

What John 3:16 is to the New Testament Church, Deuteronomy 6:4 is to the children of Israel. Under the inspiration of the Holy Spirit, Moses penned the words that would define a nation: *"**Hear, O Israel: The LORD our God is one LORD.**"* All the manipulation and massaging of this verse cannot erase the central message of the Word of God as proclaimed in this verse. God is one. He is absolutely and indivisibly one. Even a child can read and understand this verse. God is one. There is nothing complicated about or hidden in Deuteronomy 6:4. The Jews clearly understood this, the Apostles understood this, and Jesus reinforced this message during his ministry.

Mark 12:28-32 reads, *"And one of the scribes came, and having heard them reasoning together, and perceiving that he had answered them well, asked him, Which is the first commandment of all? And **Jesus answered** him, The first of all the commandments is, **Hear, O Israel; The Lord our God is one Lord**: And thou shalt love the Lord thy God with all thy heart, and with all thy soul, and with all thy mind, and with all thy strength: this is the first commandment. And the second is like, namely this, Thou shalt love thy neighbour as thyself. There is none other commandment greater than these. And the scribe said unto him, Well, Master, thou hast said the truth: **for there is one God; and there is none other but he.**"*

If there was ever a time for Jesus to enlighten the disciples and reveal to the world that he was person number two in a triune Godhead, this was the ideal opportunity. When Jesus quoted the fundamental creed of Judaism, **"Hear, O Israel: The LORD our God is one LORD;"** in one succinct statement, He reaffirmed the validity and immutability of Deuteronomy 6:4.

The implication of Jesus' words in John 8:58, *"Before Abraham was I Am,"* was not lost on the Jews. They sought to stone him for what they considered to be a blasphemous proclamation. Jesus was claiming to be the God that spoke to Moses at the burning bush, in essence, the God of Deuteronomy 6:4. Although the Jews rejected His testimony, they did understand what Jesus was saying. Jesus never pretended to be anyone other than the God of the Old Testament manifested in flesh. He never suggested that He was a lesser God, a part of God, or the Second Person of a triune Godhead.

When Jesus responded to the scribe by quoting the Shema, the scribe concurred with Him that God is one. Jesus does not dispute this fact or attempt to clear up any possible misconception the scribe may have had about the Godhead. Surely, if Jesus was part of a triune Godhead, He would have set the record straight right there. He certainly did not "beat around the bush" with Philip in John 14. When Philip asked Jesus to show him the Father, Jesus knifed to the heart of the issue, *"He that has seen Me has seen the Father!"*

When Thomas saw Jesus after the resurrection, he proclaimed, *"My Lord and my God" (John 20:28)*! Doubting Thomas doubted no more! Upon seeing the risen Savior, Thomas fell in adoration before Jesus and uttered the two most commonly used names or titles for God in the Old Testament, LORD and God. Jesus did not rebuke or correct Thomas, but rather received this great proclamation of faith and hoped aloud that others would do likewise, even if He didn't appear to them in person! Thomas finally had the revelation of the Mighty God in Christ. He recognized Jesus to be Jehovah (LORD) and Elohim (God), his Savior and Creator.

Saul of Tarsus, in Acts 9, had a similar revelation. As he traveled to Damascus to persecute those who worshiped and exalted Jesus as the One True God, he was struck from his horse and fell to the ground. Looking up into the sky, he asked after the name of the Lord: *"And he said, **Who art thou, Lord**? And **the Lord said, I am Jesus** whom thou persecutest: it is hard for thee to kick against the pricks" (Acts 9:5).* Saul persecuted the Christians with such vehemence because he so wholeheartedly rejected the notion that Jesus was the visible manifestation of the God of the Old Testament. But when he got his wake up call on the road to Damascus, he heard directly from God. Saul, *"I am Jesus!"* You are persecuting the very God you claim to serve. You are persecuting the God of Deuteronomy 6:4. Saul reversed his position and, as the Apostle Paul, announced to the world that Jesus indeed is God (Titus 2:13, Colossians 2:9-10, I Timothy 3:16). When the Apostle Paul stopped "kicking against the pricks," he received the revelation of the Mighty God in Christ. Since God is "no respecter of persons," He will do the same for you if you can put down your traditions and creeds long enough to see that the God of the Bible is One God and that His Name is Jesus.

The prayers of God's people were never uttered to a triune god. Abraham, Isaac, and Jacob prayed to one God. Joseph prayed to one God. Moses identified God as the I AM THAT I AM, not the We Are That We Are, and Moses gave Israel the Shema—our God is one. Elijah did not cry out to a plurality of persons in the Godhead on Mount Carmel. Daniel prayed to one God. Thomas realized that the God of Abraham, Isaac, Jacob, Joseph, Moses, Elijah and Daniel was none other than Jesus Christ. The Apostle Paul concurred with Thomas. Peter and John prayed for the lame man in Acts 3 in Jesus' Name—the only name given under heaven that has the power to save men (Acts 4:12). The Apostle John saw One on the throne in the Book of Revelation and identified Him as Jesus Christ (Revelation 1:8, 4:2, 4:8).

In Exodus 12:12, God made it abundantly clear that He would not share His glory with another when he pronounced that He would execute judgment against all the gods of Egypt. God never changes and a day is coming when all the false gods and all the false perceptions about God will be judged by the ONE that sits on the Throne. One day every knee will bow and every tongue will confess that Jesus Christ is Lord to the glory of God the Father (Philippians 2:10-11). How is the Father glorified through Jesus Christ? Since the Father is an invisible Spirit, He came to mankind as the Son (I Timothy 3:16, Isaiah 9:6). When a person bows to Jesus, he is bowing to the express image of the invisible God— God the Father. Jesus is the Father in flesh. Jesus is God. There is no God beside Him and we are complete in Him (Colossians 2:10).

When you say Jesus,
you have said God (Elohim).

When you say Jesus,
you have said Creator.
When you say Jesus,
you have said LORD (Jehovah).
When you say Jesus,
you have said Almighty God (El Shaddai).
When you say Jesus,
you have said Master (Adonai).
When you say Jesus,
you have said I AM THAT I AM.
When you say Jesus,
you have said Bright and Morning Star.
When you say Jesus,
you have said Sweet Rose of Sharon.
When you say Jesus,
you have said Captain of the LORD of Hosts.
When you say Jesus,
you have said Emmanuel.
When you say Jesus,
you have said Messiah.
When you say Jesus,
you have said Savior.
When you say Jesus,
you have said Lamb of God.
When you say Jesus,
you have said Good Shepherd
When you say Jesus,
you have said Alpha and Omega
When you say Jesus,
you have said Beginning and the Ending.
When you say Jesus,
you have said that which is, which was,
and which is to come.
When you say Jesus,

you have said the Light of the world.
When you say Jesus,
you have said Holy One.
When you say Jesus,
you have said Judge.
When you say Jesus,
you have said True Vine.
When you say Jesus,
you have said Father.
When you say Jesus,
you have said Son.
When you say Jesus,
you have said Holy Ghost.
**WHEN YOU SAY JESUS,
YOU HAVE SAID IT ALL!!!**

When we seek to know the Author and Finisher of our faith, we must look to Jesus, not to the manufactured gods of men's imaginations, not to philosophy, not to creeds, dogmas, and church traditions, but to Jesus alone. Jesus stated unequivocally that no man can serve two masters (Matthew 6:24). It is incomprehensible to think that God needed help being God to the extent that two additional divine persons were needed to get the job done. An old-time song writer penned the lyrics that included the expression, "one God is sufficient for me." One God is sufficient for me and Jesus is His Name!

judgment against the gods

bibliography

Adam Clark Commentary, "Ur of the Chaldeans," P.C. Study Bible, 2003 ed.

Bernard, David. *A History of Christian Doctrine, Volumes 1 & 3,* Hazelwood, MO, Word Aflame Press, 1999.

Bernard, David. *Oneness and Trinity 100-300 A.D.,* Hazelwood, MO, Word Aflame Press, 1998.

Bernard, David. *The Oneness of God,* Hazelwood, MO, Word Aflame Press, 2000.

Bowman, Robert M., et. al. *What is the Trinity and What Do Christians Believe?,* Torrance, CA, Rose Publishing, 1999.

Brown, Harold O. J. *Heresies,* Garden City, New York, Doubleday and Co., 1984.

Dake, Finnis. *Dake's Annotated Reference Bible,* Lawrencevilled, GA, Dake's Bible Sales, 1963.

Fausset, Jamieson. *Fausset's Bible Dictionary, "Zaphnathpaaneah,"* P.C. Study Bible, 2003 ed.

Fortman, E. J. *The Triune God,* Philadelphia, Westminister, 1972.

Graves, R. Brent. *The God of Two Testaments,* Hazelwood, MO, Word Aflame Press, 2000.

Huston, David. *The Light of Pentecost,* Arnold, Maryland, Antioch Publishers, 1989.

Huston, David. *The Real Message of John 3:16,* Carlisle, PA, Rosh Pinnah Publications, 1999.

Ironside, H. A. *Philippians, Colossians, Thessalonians,* Neptune, NJ, Loizeaux Brothers, 1975.

Kinzie, Fred E. *John The Gospel That Had to be Written,* Hazelwood, MO, Word Aflame Press, 1995.

Lee, Robert. *The Outlined Bible,* Grand Rapids, MI, Zondervan, 1982.

McFarland, Robert. *The History of the Origin of the Trinity,* McFarland Publishing, 2005.

Neil, T. B. *Understanding the Oneness of God,* Alberta, Canada, Page Master Publication Services Inc., 2002.

Reinhart, Fabian. *Facts for Roman Catholics,* Reinhart Publishing, 1984.

Strong, James. *Strong's Exhaustive Concordance of the Bible,* Nashville, TN, Abingdon 1980.

Tamel, Frank. *Deity In Transition,* Oak Creek, WI, Manna Ministries, 2003.

The Illustrated Bible Dictionary Volume 3, "Trinity," Wheaton, IL, Inter-Varsity Press, Tyndale House Publishers, 1980.

Urshan, Nathiel, et. al., *Symposium on Oneness Pentecostalism 1986,* Hazelwood, MO, Word Aflame Press, 1986.

Vine, W. E. *Vine's Expository Dictionary of Biblical Words,* New York, Thomas Nelson, 1980.

Willmington, H. L. *Willmington's Guide to the Bible,* Yaba, Lagos, Nigeria, Tyndale House, 1984.